THE ART CONTRIBUTION

A Companion to Living

a Meaningful Life

Ann Skinner

A Work of Heart

Copyright © 2016 by Ann Skinner

All rights reserved. No part of this book may be reproduced or copied in any form without permission from the publisher.

All illustrations by Ann Skinner

Photo by Ollie Would, Wouldland Visuals

www.TheContributionEvolution.com

ISBN-13: 978-1544750217

I dedicate this book to …

my mother, who found her vocation early in life and was an ever-present angel on my shoulder as I wrote

and

my husband, who believed in me before I did.

To Jane,

a fellow Heartworker!

much love,

Ann ♥

CONTENTS

1. CREDIT 1
2. COMMENCE 3
3. COMPONENTS 9
       COMMIT 13
       CONTRIBUTE 27
       CONNECT 61
       CREATE 91
       COMMUNICATE 123
4. CONCLUDE 145
5. CREATOR 153

1. CREDIT

THE POWER OF COMMUNITY

As I explored the subject of Contribution, I wasn't alone. I would like to take this opportunity to acknowledge my community, for being both a support and an inspiration to me. Never underestimate the power of sharing your thoughts with likeminded people as you are trying them 'out loud'.

Here are a few of their comments:

"I have probably been waiting for this moment just like you. 366 days of writing and for me 366 days of reading. I have never followed anyone with this dedication. I felt so much of me in your writing, and I also learned so much about me through your words!! Ultimately your Contribution has made me a more mindful contributor to the world! I started by giving a lot out and I am today giving a lot IN. That is my true Contribution to the world. Thank you, Ann, for this amazing journey of showing your true 'naked heart' to us and now with your book, to the world!!" – Cristina Palma, Life Coach, France.

"Your writings, words of encouragement, and just the overall energy you exude is uplifting, thoughtful, and most importantly, sincere. Thank you for being you, and thank you for your Contribution!" - Terra Bruns, Relationship Consultant, Hawaii.

"Your writing on Contribution has inspired me to make more Contributions myself and challenged my thoughts on what it all means. Contribution comes in all shapes and sizes, it wears many different clothes and can sometimes wear a disguise. It's sometimes complicated and at times just plain and simple. A massive thank you."
Liza Oxford-Booth, Training and Development Consultant, England

"In your sharing of your thoughts on Contribution I saw an alignment. When you shared, it resonated in my life and provided even more inspiration to share more. Contribution is life in the slower lane, stopping to open the garden gate, or dropping into the pub with the dog to enjoy conversation. You have taken us to a slower time and a less hard, fast and furious world, especially in the area of marketing." -
Bette Shaw, Life Coach, US

"Thank YOU Ann. I've been following quietly and reflecting silently. Your journey created inspiration for me to open up to my own journey: 365 days exploring 'creation within me'. Many thanks. What a lively Contribution!" - Emmanuelle Emande, France

2. COMMENCE

BEFORE WE BEGIN …

Dear Contributionist,

If you are reading these words, then I want to express my gratitude to you for knowing that, in a small way, I will be contributing to your life's journey.

However this book found its way to you, the very fact that it has, may very well mean that you want to be inspired to live a meaningful life. A life that contributes towards the greater good.

Why else would you choose to read a book titled The Art of Contribution?

I feel honoured to have this opportunity to share this book with you and hope the following words will help you reflect on what Contribution means to you in the context of your life.

My reflections about my own explorations into the subject have enriched my life and inadvertently, or sometimes deliberately, the lives of those around me. I hope they could do the same for you.

So welcome, dear Contributionist, as that is my term for all of us who want to purposely create more light in the world. I invite you to make a difference by being more of 'you'. To be a Leader of Light, a Light Leader if you will.

This book is an invitation for you to reflect on your own life's journey. Whilst you are reading the words that follow, I would like you to remember that there is no one way, there is only your way.

So please read my words and take what resonates and feel free to leave what isn't.

Wishing you much courage and wisdom,

Ann

HOW IT ALL BEGAN

It is only fair to tell you where my curiosity about Contribution came from. I believe it started around ten years ago, when life gave me a gift.

Sometimes life gives us gifts in ways we would rather not receive them and this was such a gift. It came to me in the form of a conflict at work, which ultimately led to me losing my job.

What this gift gave me was the gift of time. The gift of contemplation and reflection. The gift of allowing myself to feel sadness, and even anger, at the unfairness and powerlessness I felt. The gift of space to create a deeper understanding of why what happened had happened.

Although I had a good job, I had been feeling increasingly unfulfilled. I had taken the job because I knew I could do it well. I had taken the job because the company had asked me back due to my good track record, and it made me feel good to be wanted. Above all, however, I had taken the job so we could pay the bills.

There is no shame in any of that. We had just come back from extended travels and needed the security this job brought. What went wrong was that I outstayed my welcome.

I knew I hadn't been happy for a while and that unhappiness had filtered through in my work. Although I had still been putting the work in, in every other way I had been lacklustre in my participation.

A lack of purpose beyond making money kept me from feeling energised by my work and prevented me from contributing fully. I had stopped growing, felt stuck and knew I needed to create more meaning in my life.

For years my main career question had been, "What do I want to do?" This had resulted in me having a very interesting and varied career, but it hadn't necessarily always meant that my work was fulfilling. I often felt like a fraud.

The space that had opened up in my life allowed me to explore my next steps without the added pressure of worrying about the question, "What do I want to DO?"

Inspiration came to me when I changed my question and asked myself, "What do I want to BE?" It was a change of one word but that word changed my perspective forever. The answer was crystal clear to me. I wanted to be wise.

In order to be wise I needed to learn more about why we do what we do. This insight resulted in a career shift. Shortly after my revelation I moved into a new role as a sales and recruitment trainer and, in the years that followed, I started to study and eventually found my calling when I became a coach.

During this time I learned more about what motivates and inspires us to act and live the lives we choose to live. I learned that, whatever we do, at our core we all want to fulfil our basic human needs.

I learned that Contribution has the ability to fulfil us in all of our needs.

CONTRIBUTION IS …

As the years progressed, I became more and more convinced that Contribution was the route to long-lasting happiness.

However, what was Contribution? What did it really mean beyond the definition of the word? To gain a deeper understanding, I spent much of my time talking to people about what Contribution meant to them.

I even took to the streets and asked random passersby what Contribution meant from their perspective. The answers were inevitably about giving to others, i.e. giving their time or money to the community or a specific cause.

When they spoke about Contribution it was often even seen as a duty, something that we 'should' do.

My experience had taught me that, through the act of giving we create a meaningful life. However, these conversations helped me to see that there is so much more to Contribution than just giving. In fact, I found there were real challenges to be found in the act of giving.

Through my writing and sharing about what Contribution meant to me, I started to question my own beliefs around what Contribution really means.

In my explorations, I came to realise that there is an Art to Contribution.

Ann Skinner

3. COMPONENTS

THE HEART OF CONTRIBUTION

As I sat down and went through a year's worth of writing, scribbled notes and thoughts about my explorations on the Art of Contribution, I noticed some common themes.

These themes were like components that fit together, although in no particular order, with each part holding and amplifying the other:

Commit. Contribute. Connect. Create. Communicate.

They reminded me of the five elements of Ayurveda, one of the world's oldest holistic healing systems, which believes that everything in this universe is made up of five great elements of building blocks. These are fire, air, earth, water and ether. On their own they do not support life, but together they create the magic of our existence.

COMMIT - we need a fire in our belly. A fire to get us past the fear and allow us to leap beyond our comfort zone to a place of growth and expansion.

CONTRIBUTE - we need the air to sustain us. We can't breathe out without breathing in and we can't breathe in without breathing out. In the same way, there is no give without receive and there is no receive without give.

CONNECT - we need the earth to ground ourselves, to reconnect us to our inner being so we can connect to others from a place of presence and grace.

CREATE - we need to be fluid, like water, and allow our creativity to flow effortlessly to and from us. We can create a life that either pushes upstream or flows downstream.

COMMUNICATE - we need to be aware that our very essence is like the ether - it's more than what our eyes can see. We are the energy that makes up our universe and have the power to create or destroy.

BEFORE WE CONTINUE

The five components of *Commit, Contribute, Connect, Create* and *Communicate* will gently hold the content of my musings. They are not a 'how to' but a reflector to help you consider what it means for you to live an authentic and meaningful life.

Each component offers an introductory lead-in, followed by a number of separate stories. These stories are my contemplations on what Contribution meant to me in the context of my exploration. They are no more than a personal reflection of my innermost thoughts on a specific subject at a particular time and place.

The Art of Contribution

Whilst writing and editing this book, I noticed how my energy felt different for each component. I found that there were some elements that flowed naturally for me, whilst others clearly showed my discomfort. It would have been only too easy to have chosen to rewrite these parts but I believe that, in the rewriting, these segments would have lost their honesty and power. The power of vulnerability.

As you are reading each chapter, you may want to check in with your own reactions and ask yourself, "Are they a reflection of my thoughts about what the writer is saying, or are my thoughts and feelings perhaps a mirror of what is going on in my own life?"

It is very much my wish that, after you have read this book, it will continue to be a source of reference for you. A place for reflection and inspiration in any given moment.

If any of my insights help you to gain yours, this book will have served its purpose.

The writing of it has already been life changing for me.

♥

As you read on, you will find each story punctuated by a heart symbol. This is your cue to take a moment of reflection before moving on.

♥

Ann Skinner

COMMIT

We need a fire in our belly. A fire to get us past the fear and allow us to leap beyond our comfort zone to a place of growth and expansion.

I COMMIT

In order to live a meaningful life, I wanted to own what I really, truly stood for. So I asked myself, if I had a message for the world, what would it be?

When it came down to it, I knew I stood for 'Contribution'. "That's great," I heard people say as I shared my message, "But what does that really mean? Why is this message so important to you and what does that mean for me personally?" When I tried to explain it, I came a little unstuck.

Why? Because it meant so many things on so many levels.

I believed in the power of choosing to live a meaningful life.

I knew I believed in how much contributing to someone else's happiness increases our own.

I believed that there would be more value in judging the success of a business on its meaningful impact, rather than just how much profit it makes.

I also believed that it is only too easy to contribute at our own expense.

I, therefore, believed that we need to learn how to contribute sustainably, in a way that works for both us and the greater good.

I also believed that whatever message we feel urged to share with the world, our Contribution if you like, is often something that we have had to learn along the way.

Still, explaining the 'how' or 'why' of it in a way that made sense to others remained challenging for me. All I knew was that if I didn't follow my calling, I would feel deeply unhappy.

So I decided to commit to understanding what my belief meant for me and why I felt this was so important. For a whole year I decided to 'stand for Contribution' by exploring and writing about the subject daily.

This commitment was a catalyst for many insights and allowed me to stretch myself to new levels.

Reflect ♥ Recalibrate ♥ Read on

THE PROMISE

Although I had promised myself that I would write a post about Contribution every single day for a year, there were times when I just didn't feel like doing it.

Some days I would know exactly what to write about; some days I had a vague idea of an angle; but there were also times when I sat down in front of the computer with no idea at all. A number of times I would question my sanity and wondered if I really needed to stick so rigidly to 'my promise'. Surely it would be nice to go on holiday and just take a break for a few days? What harm would it do?

Taking consistent action of any kind is a challenge, and as soon as these thoughts crept into my consciousness I knew I was in trouble. If I let these thoughts take hold, my inner demons would start to find ways of sabotaging my good intentions. So why did I stick with it?

Because I had made a commitment to myself to do so.

Because this commitment made me determined and helped me to get past my fears, past my need for perfection. It helped me to focus instead on creating an opportunity for the inspiration I needed to visit me.

Because consistency creates resilience against resistance. I started to trust that my inspiration would come. It always did and I learned to just wait with my fingers at the ready until it happened. Like magic, something would drift into my peripheral vision, some small thought or phrase that I could latch onto and expand on.

Because I knew why I had made the promise to myself. I wanted to learn more about my subject. I wanted to create something worthy to me. I wanted to create and share something of value to myself and others. I wanted to practice my craft.

Because I knew that, if I did not keep this promise to myself, I would feel disappointed in myself. As they say – there is either do or don't, there is no in between.

Because I shared my commitment with others and that promise helped me to stay accountable to myself.

Because I had the support of my loved ones, in particular my husband, who kept me on track when I was feeling a little wobbly.

Because I left myself choice. It was never a 'should' – always a choice. My choice.

Writer Paulo Coelho once wrote, "What is success? It is going to bed each night with your soul at peace." I knew my soul was at peace when I honoured my commitment.

Honouring this commitment has been my biggest Contribution to myself to date and, through it, I have had the great fortune and honour of having been able to contribute to many others.

Contribution is honouring a promise to yourself.

♥

TAKING A STAND

A friend once said, "When we take a stand, people think you automatically stand against something else."

This got me thinking about standing for or against something. When you stand for peace, for example, do you automatically stand against war? I am not sure that is always true; however, I do feel there is a difference of focus.

It reminded me of a rally my husband and I were inspired to join. It was a rally to protest against the bombing of Syria. I had never protested before. Well, perhaps to going to bed too early, but never for something that mattered, out on the streets, in the rain.

It was a small group, as there hadn't been much publicity for the event. Those there, however, were very friendly and it was an interesting bunch. Some die-hard anarchists, some political activists who went to rallies every week, some who were supporting the opposition party and a few like me, who felt that they needed to do something to let their voices be heard.

I was glad I had gone, but I had felt a little uncomfortable and out of place. It was as if my energy was being pulled in the wrong direction. The direction of 'what I don't want' rather than 'what I do want'.

This experience had made me realise that I personally do not want to fight AGAINST anything. Instead I prefer to stand FOR something.

The difference between the two may seem small, but they feel like chalk and cheese to me.

Contribution is standing for something, rather than against something.

♥

THE COURAGE OF OUR HEART

How often do we get stopped by our fears?

We think about things and then we think some more, and the more we think about it, the more fear creeps in. The more fear creeps in, the less courageous we feel and when we start to lose our courage we find ways of sabotaging ourselves.

I went back to one of my favourite books, *The War of Art*, by Steven Pressfield, for some inspiration, as it shares great wisdom around the subject of resistance.

Pressfield reminded me of the rule of thumb, "The more important a call or action is to our soul's evolution, the more Resistance we will feel toward pursuing it." This rang true for me, as our fear of failure increases the moment the stakes are high.

We create stories in our head and focus on whether we are good enough, strong enough, experienced enough or know enough. What these stories have in common is that they focus on what we don't want rather than what we do want, and focussing on what we don't want creates fear - fear that stops us from moving forward.

Through my work with my clients I am so often reminded that love conquers fear and that courage lives in our heart, not our head.

"You lose your sense of fear thinking of other people." A beautiful quote by a war veteran in a speech at the centenary commemorations of the battle of the Somme about jumping out of the trenches into battle.

Not that I want to glorify war, but the message I take away is that being other-focussed gives us courage beyond what we ever thought would be possible.

The moment we put our focus outside of ourselves, to a cause greater than ourselves, we find the courage we need to take the next step forward.

My promise to my community and my promise to my clients kept me on track and gave me the courage and conviction to lead with my heart and my head.

Courage + Conviction = Growth

Contribution is having the courage of your convictions.

♥

DUTCH COURAGE

Over the years many people have labelled me as courageous.

In that time I have also learned that courage is only a question of perspective. Many things I have done in my life didn't take courage for me. For example:

Moving abroad on my own when I was 19.

Starting jobs without really knowing whether I would be able to do them.

Setting up a business in a recession.

Sailing halfway around the world, past Cape Horn and through the Southern Ocean.

Selling and starting up again countless of times.

At all of those times it wasn't courage that took me, it was excitement, exhilaration and ignorance; as in ignorance is bliss! I had no idea what lay ahead and that idea was fun rather than frightening to me.

Most of the time, a belief that all would work out for the best got me through. And, yes, mostly it did.

However, there was one area in my life where I lacked courage. I knew how to be tough, strong and daring, but I didn't know how to be vulnerable.

For me the act of being vulnerable takes far more courage. Like so many of us, the fear of being good enough as 'just me' was strong in me. Committing to myself, and to a cause greater than myself, forced me to start learning to be courageous in this area too.

This journey has taught me the importance of showing up fully at times when I might be judged about something personal and important to me. I learned to be more courageous about sharing my heartfelt creations, my true thoughts and showing who I was beyond the facade, beyond identity, beyond critical thought.

Contribution is allowing ourselves to be vulnerable.

♥

COMMITMENT MATTERS

I read a fantastic article by writer Mark Manson. In it Manson argues that, if you find yourself sweating the small stuff, you obviously haven't found something 'fuckworthy' enough yet. Strong language, I know, but he makes a good point.

We sometimes forget that we can choose what we care about. Do we care about the fact that the top is off the toothpaste, or do we care about something truly important to us? (Thankfully the toothpaste issue is never a problem in our household and, sadly, I just realised I might actually care if it were!)

I wondered about where am I still sweating the small stuff and where am I still holding back and worrying about what other people think? Too many instances, I am afraid to admit. But I have started to see a shift in myself ever since I decided to commit to what I stand for.

Of course, there is a fine line between being indifferent and not worrying about something because you have a cause greater than yourself to worry about. In other words, it is not about learning not to care, it is about learning what to care about. The words integrity and resilience pop up for me here.

This also reminded me of another Manson article titled, *7 strange questions that help you find your life purpose*. I have particularly enjoyed asking my clients one of these questions in my workshops: "What is your favourite flavour of shit sandwich and does it come with an olive?" In other words, what are you willing to sacrifice?

I love this question. Apart from the fact that it is a brilliant question in its own right, it is also poignant as it is a great measure of our commitment to our cause.

What are you willing to sacrifice to make it happen? Will you be prepared to fail? Will you be prepared to be rejected for what you believe in? Will you be prepared to stop sweating the small stuff? Will you be prepared to stay up until the middle of the night writing the daily post you've committed to, even when your eyes are grainy and your brain feels mushy?!?

Living 'on purpose' may be fulfilling, but it comes at a cost too. Surely, therefore, it is best to know what we are making our sacrifices for?

Challenging or not, I personally would rather live my life on purpose, than find myself on my deathbed, wondering, "Now what was the purpose of that!"

Contribution is being prepared to make sacrifices for what you believe in.

♥

DIVIDING TIME

My biggest challenge remained my focus, which tended to flit between my work for my coaching practice and my voluntary work. They were so intertwined, but one was meant to create a sustainable income.

There were two things I learned here. One was about the way I was working and the other about the way I was thinking.

Firstly, I felt my lack of focus on one or the other created no satisfaction either way. I needed to 'chunk' my time better. Rather than doing little bits here and there, I needed to be clear on what I was doing when.

One of the inspirations for this decision was some research I read. It looked into how people feel about their impact if their voluntary work is scattered over the week, rather than being focused in set chunks. It turns out that chunking our activities in blocks of time creates a greater feeling of having made a difference.

Secondly, and not unimportantly, it made me realise that I didn't think about my paid coaching work as 'Contribution' in the same way as I was thinking about my unpaid work.

Apparently, at some stage I had decided that the moment I get paid for something, it isn't Contribution.

By committing to clearer actions and by challenging my beliefs around what constitutes Contribution, I will be able to start identifying where and how I can make a bigger difference. Both to my own life and to the lives of those around me.

Contribution is feeling that your actions have made a difference.

♥

DOING THE WORK

We are often told to just get on with it. Resistance is just something to work through.

I want to say, no!!! I don't want to do the work! I want to play and not have to do grown up stuff. I want to dance in the woods, chat to friends, laugh, sing and be merry and not worry about having to do 'the work'.

The funny thing is, however, I love my work. Through my work I feel I can make a real difference. When work becomes challenging for me is when I get bogged down with 'making it work'.

There are, however, times when we have to knuckle down and 'do the work'. This is where having a commitment to ourselves and to something greater than ourselves creates leverage.

Finding a cause bigger than ourselves allows us to overcome our mental block and helps us to get past our resistance.

Contribution is doing the work.

♥

CHOOSE YOUR VALUES

Einstein said, "Try not to become a man of success, but a man of value."

I often work with my clients on their values and what those values stand for. After all, what we value determines our direction in life. The meaning we give to those values and how we execute them will determine how we feel about life.

Committing to our values and what they stand for is a powerful thing.

In a speech I once listened to, a young Nigerian lady shared the three values she was brought up with, the three Rs: Respect for yourself, Respect for others and Responsibility for all that you do.

Such simple values and at the same time so potent. What I found interesting about these values is that it starts with Respect for yourself and ends with Responsibility for all we do. How often are we taught to respect others and to put ourselves down? How often do we take responsibility for others and forget to take responsibility for ourselves?

We are all human and capable of extreme acts of hatred, as well as extreme acts of love. What drives one or the other if not our values?

Nelson Mandela reminded us that, "No one is born with hatred in their heart." He taught us that hatred breeds more hatred and love more love.

Mandela also taught us that love doesn't mean giving in; love means standing up for what you believe in, without compromising your integrity and without running away from the fear of the consequences.

Sometimes we need to relearn what our heart already knows.

Contribution is committing to love above all else.

♥

CONTRIBUTE

We need the air to sustain us. We can't breathe out without breathing in and we can't breathe in without breathing out. In the same way, there is no give without receive and there is no receive without give.

I CONTRIBUTE

Something really clicked in me when I was introduced to a book called *Give and Take*, by Adam Grant. He looked at what made people successful in business. However, I believe what he found also translates to life in general.

Grant looked beyond the normal success indicators of hard work, talent and luck. He found there was one other ingredient which was key. Our success depends heavily on how we approach our interactions with other people. How much value do we create and who for? Do we want to give and/or take?

With my explorations around the Art of Contribution this was naturally very interesting to me.

When Grant researched how we behave in business, he noticed that there were a number of ways in which people operate. He was able to categorise people as either givers, takers or matchers.

As a brief explanation, givers are those who want to create value for others; takers are those who want to create value for themselves; and matchers are those who want to create value for others but only if they get the same value in return.

When looking at who were the most successful, he found that, although matchers were reasonably successful, takers were the most successful in the short run. Givers were the most successful in the long run, however - and this was the key thing that I learned - givers were both at the TOP of the tree and the BOTTOM of the tree.

This was fascinating to me. What was it that separated the top level givers from the bottom level?

What I learned opened my eyes and taught me more about the other side of Contribution, i.e. what makes it sustainable.

Reflect ♥ Recalibrate ♥ Read on

GULLIBLE OR GRACEFUL

Adam Grant's book, *Give and Take*, taught me that there are three main things that separate the givers at the top and the givers at the bottom. First, the top layer of givers knew how to receive; second, they were clear about what they wanted to give; and third they were aware of when they were able to give it.

I now refer to the top and bottom level givers as, respectively, the 'graceful givers' and the 'gullible givers'.

Through my explorations on the subject, I have been in contact with a large number of heart-centred people all over the world who have struggled to make an income doing what they love doing. Why? Because they like to give, as in give away. Many fall into the category 'gullible givers', rather than 'graceful givers'.

What is clear from my conversations is that, apart from having a giving mindset, the thing that 'gullible givers' have in common is that they are not able to be clear on either their receiving or giving boundaries. Too often they leave themselves out of the equation. It pains me to say it, but I realised that at some level I had to include myself in this category.

Journalist and writer Irma Kurtz, the mother of all agony aunts, once said, "Givers have to set limits because takers rarely do." This is why, when a giver is paired with a taker they can find themselves in trouble, although let's face it, we are also perfectly capable of getting ourselves into trouble!

Of course, we are never just one thing as our approach will depend on each situation, but most of us have a default setting and it is this setting that influences our life's perspective. A setting that can be changed, however, if we are prepared to do some inner work.

Contribution is being clear on our giving and receiving boundaries.

♥

THE GIVER'S TRAP - THE PROCRASTINATOR

A big trap that givers fall into is overcommitting themselves. Givers hate disappointing people when asked for help, and also tend to offer their services where they feel they can help. Unfortunately, this often results in the realisation that they don't have time to take care of their own responsibilities without overstretching themselves.

Something always suffers. Sometimes it means not being able to follow up on promises, to ourselves or others. Sometimes it means not spending time with loved ones. Sometimes it means working late into the night to finish off our own work.

Looking back, this has been a fairly common occurrence throughout my life. First at school and later at work, I was only too happy to be distracted by questions from others, so I could support them and put my own work off. It never seemed quite as important as theirs and helping them made me feel good. Procrastination posing as Contribution perhaps?

The problem was that, at the end of the day, my work was still there to be done. It meant I stayed late. Often. Too often. Of course I would never ask for help myself.

Classic 'gullible giver' type behaviour.

Recently, I have been learning to say 'no' to others when I realise I am overcommitting myself. However, I still find it hard to say 'no' to myself, when I put pressure on myself by creating unrealistic expectations.

Sustainability goes hand in hand with Contribution. It is about knowing our boundaries. It is about self-care. It is about being intelligent about how we show up in the world.

Contribution is having the ability to say no by recognising our priorities.

♥

WORK LIFE BALANCE

Is there such a thing as a work life balance? I have always been of the belief that work is part of life, so how can you separate the two? The moment we do is the moment we get into trouble.

What I have come to realise is that it isn't a question of achieving a work life balance, but more a question of achieving a balance between give and receive.

If I think back to when I got tired or dissatisfied at work, I was either giving too much, i.e. my time, my expertise, my efforts, or I was not giving what I wanted to give. Both were depleting my energies.

Thinking about other times when I felt out of sync at work, I felt that I did not receive sufficiently compared to what I put in. And I don't just mean financially, although that is of course important, but it may have been on an intellectual, emotional or spiritual level. There were times when I was lacking appreciation, or feeling like I didn't belong, and times when I wasn't being stretched enough.

Whatever it was, the imbalance was always between what I gave and what I received. Of course, life is never totally in balance all the time, but it helps to create awareness about what contributes to our wellbeing.

Contribute. To. Our. Wellbeing. This is hugely important when we talk about sustainability. Giving AND receiving. We have an energy bank and if it gets depleted we cannot sustain our giving.

I believe that thinking of it this way helps us to consciously think more clearly about where we are crossing our boundaries.

Contribution is creating a sustainable balance of give and receive.

♥

GIVING VERSUS GIVING AWAY

Of course life is filled with compromises, but where do we compromise ourselves in the process? When is a compromise a compromise too far?

How often do we find ourselves saying 'yes' to a request from a family member, friend or colleague, when we really want to say 'no'? Are we afraid to say 'no' for fear of upsetting them; do we say 'yes' out of a sense of duty; or do we say yes because we want to?

When should we put ourselves first and when should we put ourselves out for someone else when it is actually inconvenient to us? How do we distinguish between the times that it is right to do so, and the times it isn't?

These are all questions around knowing our boundaries. What has helped me to gain clarity on my boundaries is knowing what I want and why I want it. The 'why', in particular, has helped me to figure out what is right or wrong for me at any given time.

I realised that to know if I was off-track or not, it helped to check in with my emotional guidance system, and ask myself how a particular decision made me feel. Did it make me feel good or bad to say 'yes' or 'no'?

This may sound like a fairly simple measure, and I appreciate that simple doesn't always mean easy.

I thought about this some more as I sat waiting in the hospital for my husband, who was having some tests done. It was very 'inconvenient' for me to be there but there was no question in my mind that I wanted to be there. To not support him would have compromised my integrity and my love for him.

So, of course, there are times when it is appropriate to put ourselves second. It is most definitely part of the ebb and flow of giving and receiving in life and the difference between being sustainable or self-centred.

Another memory comes to mind. One night I was in a nearby city for an event and I noticed the amount of homeless people. A few came up to me for some spare change, which I gave.

On the way home the same happened and I started feeling some discomfort around it. I decided that I could not continue to just give, as my giving was turning into 'giving away'. I felt I had reached my limit and was about to go over my boundaries.

I wasn't quite sure what I was going to say to the next person who would ask. I felt that I couldn't just say, "No, not tonight", and I certainly couldn't just ignore them. Instead, I decided to be honest about how I felt, i.e. that I would love to help, but that I was starting to get a little concerned that I couldn't keep saying 'yes' as that wouldn't be sustainable for me.

The person I explained this to immediately told me that it was no problem at all, that I had 'done my bit' and that was all that could be asked of me. He gave me permission to be ok with saying 'no', to put myself first and to appreciate that we do what we can, when we can.

At the end of the day, we can only give of ourselves honestly, in the moment.

Contribution is giving, without giving yourself away.

♥

FOR THE GREATER GOOD

What if we are on this earth purely to help ourselves? That instead of believing we could learn to give more, we started believing we could learn to receive more? Like some of you, this thought brings up all sorts of resistance and, still, I wonder about it. Hear me out.

When we are talking about Contribution, we mostly think of it as serving others, but actually we are serving ourselves. To a 'giver' that feels extremely uncomfortable. "It isn't about us!" we say. But you know what? It is every bit about us.

When I was supporting charity staff during a workshop, I caught them complaining about businesses who had reacted to their request for support with the question, "What's in it for us?"

It created an interesting discussion, as I argued that everything we do, we do in order to satisfy our own needs at some level. We are wired that way. Businesses too.

Even when we do things for others, we ultimately do it because it makes us feel good, because it connects us to others and/or ourselves, gives us a sense of belonging and feeds us with a sense of certainty and even significance.

So the "What's in it for me?" question isn't a bad one to check in with. It is when we forget to ask this question that we can forget our boundaries. Many of the people in that workshop were constantly over-stretching themselves.

Again, I wondered, how would it change things if we were able to learn to receive more of all life has to offer? Would we not be able to give even more as a result? Isn't Contribution about serving our true selves, who we really are? Not from an ego perspective, but from the perspective of serving our higher purpose?

So, perhaps instead of asking ourselves, "How can I serve others?" we may be better off asking ourselves, "How can I best serve my higher purpose?" From that place we might have a better chance of creating a sustainable life.

It's a balance of Contribution being all about others, whilst it is also all about us.

Contribution is working for the greater good of all (and that includes us).

♥

ENOUGH IS ENOUGH

In a conversation with a friend we discussed a question she was once asked, "When do you know you have given enough?"

This question kept playing in the back of my mind long after our conversation. Perhaps it was because I was struggling with an infection, which had been slumbering for a while and was sucking all my energy, but really, when is enough, enough?

There have been many times in my life when I have been hard on myself and often bashed myself over the head when I felt tired. "Come on, Ann, just get on with it!" I would be telling myself. "You should be able to do more than you are doing! Some people have three children, run a couple of businesses and then also find time to work with a couple of charities! What the heck are you doing?"

The thing is, it is so easy to compare ourselves to others and worry about whether we are doing enough. I have really started to question the value of comparing ourselves in such a way, as there is always someone who appears to be able to do more or less than us at any given time. Surely our ability to 'do' is different for all of us at different times.

Going back to the question, "When do you know you have given enough?", the word 'enough' in this context made me wonder if, when we think of giving, we tend to measure the amount rather than the quality. Which makes me think, what we are really doing is making sure we *are* enough by *doing* enough.

Mother Theresa was quoted as saying, "It's not how much we give, but how much love we put into giving." It serves as a great reminder that it isn't about how much we give, but about where we are giving from. When we are our loving, authentic selves, we are already giving more than enough.

The key then, perhaps, is knowing that whatever we do, we are always enough. We don't have to do anything, give anything, be anything to ever be enough.

Contribution is being no more or less than your loving self.

♥

THE POWER OF GIVING

There is power in giving, but perhaps not all of it is directed in the way we would like to think.

Giving makes us feel good. Why? Because it feeds our basic human needs, such as our sense of significance, our feelings of connection and our need to make a difference. This makes the act of giving such a powerful one.

However, the thing with giving is that it can go two ways. While it can make us feel good about ourselves, it can also be either enabling or disabling for the receiver. So creating some consciousness around this might not be a bad thing.

Looking back, I can see many examples where I may have inadvertently disabled, rather than enabled, someone with my 'help'.

What I have come to recognise is that our emotional guidance system will usually tell us which of the two is in action. When the giving is followed with a sense of dissatisfaction, from either side, it is likely to have been disabling.

Usually, it is because we have either tried to help someone who hasn't asked for help and isn't ready to receive it, or we have given support to someone who is only too happy to accept help without taking any responsibility for their own actions. In both cases our 'help' keeps them where they are.

Help given in this way feeds their belief that at some level they are not capable of helping themselves. This is obviously the opposite of our original intention, which was to support and empower them. Just having a positive intention, however, isn't always enough.

Often the best help we can offer is the gift of our love and our presence.

Contribution is empowering others to help themselves by believing they can.

♥

HELP I'M A HELPER!

I read the book *Big Magic*, by Elizabeth Gilbert, in which she writes about many things that I recognise and resonate with.

Not least of these is a quote by British columnist Katharine Whitehorn, "You can recognise the people who live for others by the haunted look on the faces of the others."

That sentence stayed with me for a long time, because I recognised myself, and not necessarily in a good way. It reminded me of some of the faces that have looked back at me throughout my life, as I was trying to 'help' without invitation.

I have matured somewhat, but I still catch myself out plenty of times. Often too late! Occasionally I see such a face looking back at me and I realise that I am 'doing it again'. Helping without being asked to do so.

Many of us love to help. When we are the helper we are in control and that makes us feel good. The problem is that our help might come with a hidden agenda and that can create some challenges, particularly as we often aren't even aware we have an agenda.

Reflecting back on those situations, what I often really wanted, besides helping someone to feel better, was not to have to watch a situation whilst feeling powerless to do anything. I didn't want to feel powerless; I wanted to help fix what was going wrong, so that we could have some fun again.

The result of this so-called help was not always very helpful. When I see someone's eyes glaze over I now know I have crossed the line again.

It has also become much clearer to me that having an agenda is not necessarily the problem, as long as we're open about it. By sharing our agenda we are, in effect, turning the tables, because by doing so we are asking them to help us by helping themselves! Such a lovely paradox.

When 'helping' is our default setting, we might be well advised to learn to know where the off switch is, or recalibrate the setting to helping the helper instead, i.e. yourself!

Contribution is offering help WITH permission.

♥

TRUTH AND COURAGE

A lifetime spent being independent and self-reliant meant that asking for help was a skill I hadn't started to develop until recently. To some extent, I still struggle with this today.

Asking for help is an important part of our ability to receive. So, as part of my commitment to myself, I decided to learn more about the art of asking for help. As a result I accepted a 30-day challenge, where every day I had to ask for help in whatever way I wanted and for whatever I wanted help with.

What I found was that it was the hardest and most uncomfortable thing I have ever had to do. My lack of practice meant that I did not know 1) what to ask for help with and 2) how to ask for help gracefully.

This challenge taught me a very valuable lesson about the difference between give and receive.

When we give help we tend to be in control. When we ask for help, however, we are required to be open, meaning we have to let go of control. This feels scary and very vulnerable.

The truth about vulnerability is that it takes courage, even though it feels like weakness. As social researcher and writer Brené Brown says, "Vulnerability sounds like truth and feels like courage. Truth and courage aren't always comfortable, but they are never weakness."

Contribution is allowing others to help you.

♥

THE PRACTICE OF RECEIVING

Three quarters of the year into exploring the art of Contribution I celebrated my fiftieth birthday. This gave me plenty of practice in the art of receiving.

Presents, warm wishes and compliments winged their way to me in abundance.

It taught me that I have become more than capable of receiving graciously, without the need to reciprocate. In fact, I am now able to own up to the fact that I rather enjoy receiving.

At the same time, I learned another lesson.

For a few years, I had subtly implied to my husband that my right hand was rather empty and that it would be nice 'perhaps' to have a lovely ring on it 'one day'.

Several birthdays and a couple of other landmarks, like our 20th, 21st and 22nd wedding anniversary (all very good opportunities, I thought) passed and still no ring.

It was not that my husband wasn't listening, nor that he didn't want to buy me one, but he never quite knew what to get me. "Jewellery is not my forte," he would say.

This time, I decided to make my request more explicit. "Neil, I would love to have a special ring for my fiftieth birthday. Would that be alright? I would be happy to choose one myself."

"Yes of course," was the answer, "Shall we pick one together?" Problem solved and everybody happy, including my husband, who can find the act of buying gifts a little stressful.

It was so simple. I just had to ask for it straight out! A number one rule in sales is not to beat about the bush when you are asking for what you want. I sometimes wonder if I ever listened to myself when I used to deliver my sales training and coaching sessions!

There is a sense of peace and freedom in the ability to ask for what you want and to receive gracefully.

Contribution is the ability to ask and receive with grace.

♥

AFFIRMING ABUNDANCE

How to give, whilst being fearful about not having enough, is a challenge many of us face.

Whilst in the shower one day, I reflected that abundance is not about having, but about being. We are abundant the moment we feel abundant.

A simple thought came to me that helped put some of my fears around feeling that I was lacking to bed.

"I will always have enough."

Then after some reflection I rephrased it to,

"I will always have more than enough," because, after all, enough is just enough, and I wondered if that would be enough …

Although close, it still hadn't quite hit the spot for me, and whilst continuing with my ablutions, another thought came to me,

"I will always have more than enough to share."

This felt right. After all, having is just about ourselves, and sharing is about both of us. It seemed an important distinction.

A simple affirmation which gives me the strength to trust that all will be well, if I just keep contributing what I love doing.

This small mantra puts me in a space of abundance and keeps my fears at bay. "I always have more than enough to share" refers to time, money or any resource where I might be challenged by a feeling that I'm somehow lacking.

It helps me to come back to myself, to be present to the knowledge that I am abundant the moment I feel abundant.

Contribution is feeling abundant regardless of circumstance.

♥

FANNING THE FLAME

At a networking event I found myself listening to a very entertaining speech about the heart and soul of volunteering. You can imagine that I was all ears.

The lovely gentleman who spoke shared, most enthusiastically, about how for most of his life he'd spent his spare time volunteering. From early childhood he was involved in charitable work. After a career in the ambulance service he finally took over as Fundraising Manager for a large cancer charity. His dream job.

He shared how, throughout his life, any spare time he had he would devote to supporting some cause. Whether that was helping out at school, coaching at the local rugby team, volunteering at a music festival, or helping the elderly.

All of us who were witness to his speech were tired just thinking about everything he had managed to do over the years. He, on the other hand, sparkled. Volunteering lifted his heart and soul.

My first thoughts were of how tired I would be if I had done all he did. My second thought was that I 'should' do a little more volunteering too. Finally came the awareness that this was just my old habit of judging myself by comparing myself with others.

On reflection, I realised that what he had been talking about mostly was everything he had gained from volunteering. Free tickets to concerts and games, but above all the people he had met and the fun he had had through these connections and events. He gave much and received much in return. Volunteering made him come alive. In fact, it had shaped his life.

It highlighted something again for me. Ultimately, the best charitable work we can do is the very thing that lights us up. This may not necessarily be 'volunteering', although it can be.

It reminded me of what Three Principles educator, Dicken Bettinger, said at an event, "Fan the flame inside of you until that flame bursts into flame."

This man's flame was bursting. Mine would have been extinguished if I had walked the same path. We all have to follow our own light.

Contribution is sharing that which lights you up.

♥

SERVING THE WORLD

My husband is an avid runner and is part of a local running club. I often come along as a supporter, being happy to stand on the sidelines cheering him on.

The Art of Contribution

We were once asked to pick up a woman called Josie on the way to a local running event. This 92 year old veteran is a legend in the running club. As we chatted to Josie, we soon realised she isn't just a legend in the running club. Josie is a legend. Full stop.

Josie was a long distance runner and a world record holder. She could still run a marathon at well under four hours at the age of 71. This year, at 92 and after a triple bypass, she still managed a 5 kilometre race, handed out all the prizes and stayed till late into the evening, despite the blaring music.

It was clear that Josie is in love with life and loves sharing it with likeminded people. She found her passion and chose, against the odds, to pursue it. Josie played a key role in the local running club for 30+ years and you could see the love people had for her.

She has been an inspiration for many, not only because of everything she has done for others, but mostly for everything she has done for herself. Isn't that the best Contribution we can give?

Josie hadn't set out to create a legacy. She just pursued the one thing that made her come alive.

Another legend of a similar ilk is Sister Madonna Buder, known as the Iron Lady, who, at 82, was the oldest person to ever finish an Ironman Triathlon. She started running at 48 and completed her first triathlon at 52, after "training religiously." What an inspiration!

In an interview Sister Madonna Buder shared her thoughts about what she believe to be our purpose in life:

To change the world that you are in. To give to the world what you have. To serve the world with who you are.

The real key, for me, lies in number three. Do the inner work to do the outer work. Learn about who you truly are at your core and share your passions for the greater good. If you then happen to win a couple of world records in the process, it's a nice bonus!

Contribution is serving the world with who you are.

♥

THE BUSINESS OF CONTRIBUTION

Being a coach for me is first and foremost about making a difference. However, second, I would like to make a good living from it so I am able to do more of it.

When your work is your vocation, it can be a challenge to accept money for what you feel comes naturally to you, even though you might have spent thousands of pounds on honing this natural ability!

This is a struggle I have encountered in many people. That critical voice at the back of your mind that tells you that it is wrong to receive money for doing the very thing that you love doing. Particularly as you would be just as happy if you gave it away, however, that would not be sustainable.

I was once asked, "When does Contribution become business?" In other words, when do you stop giving away and start receiving, i.e. getting paid money for what you do?

An interesting question and it gave me the insight that, even when we are paid for our service, our level of Contribution never goes down –

the only difference is that the level of receiving goes up. Sometimes, although I hasten to add not always, it also means that the perceived value for the service or product you offer goes up.

This question helped me to remember something I had forgotten. Giving has nothing to do with receiving money or not receiving money. In fact, writer and journalist William Carpenter once wrote, "There is no separation between giving and receiving" and I think this is true. There is no separation unless we choose to separate the two by not allowing one or the other to flow through us.

Whether we are paid or not depends on a number of things. First, the value we create as well as the value we give our service or product. Second, what others believe it is worth to them. Third, how much what we give feeds us, whether spiritually, emotionally, physically and/or financially.

I read an interesting perspective by writer Rebecca Campbell regarding the last point. In her book, *Light is the New Black*, she gets us to ask ourselves, "What do you need to do the work you need to do?" In other words, what do you need from the universe in order to create a sustainable life for yourself? A life where you feel safe, nurtured and cared for, so you can continue to do the things that you are meant to do.

This helped me to formulate more clearly what it is I need in order to create a life that is both fulfilling and sustainable at the same time.

Contribution is being in the business of giving and receiving.

♥

ABOUT GIVING AND GETTING

"Don't give to get. Give to inspire others to give," a beautiful quote by Simon Sinek, a well-known author, speaker and management consultant.

It reminded me of a conversation I had with a businessman at a local network meeting earlier this year. I was sharing my fascination with the subject of Contribution and how giving enriches our lives.

"Yes," was his response, "Give to get." This response gave me pause for thought and rang in my head for a long time afterwards. It made me realise that the moment I think of giving in order to get, it becomes weird in my mind. Still, I know this is what we do all the time.

When we relate this to business, it is a simple and effective marketing strategy to entice people with 'give-aways' in order to get them ultimately to buy your product. I myself give my time, for example, which allows someone an experience of me so they can decide whether I am the right coach for them and I can decide if they are the right client for me.

This makes perfect sense, and yet, I felt uncomfortable by his comment. In the end, I realised what it was that made me feel so uncomfortable. For me, the energy behind the giving does make a difference.

How often have I been given free sample products in my lifetime? I freely admit that I like to receive them, but at the same time, I also find a sense of greed bubbling up in me. It is weird. I definitely don't feel 'inspired to give'; in fact, I feel inspired to 'get more'.

Give to inspire people to give means exactly that – you inspire them to either give back to you, whether through buying your product or doing something nice for you, or you inspire them to give something of themselves to someone else; and that might even be giving back to themselves.

I realised the difference was ultimately this - when we give to get, we put ourselves at the centre, whereas when we give to inspire to give, our focus is outward. Perhaps it is the difference between a taker's versus a (graceful) giver's mentality.

Contribution is being inspired to give and get.

♥

A SUSTAINABLE BUSINESS

Over and over again I have heard people say that business is ultimately all about increasing the bottom line. Because, they argue, if you don't increase the bottom line, you'll find your business won't be sustainable.

Although there is obvious truth in this message, it also puts the focus squarely on money as the measure of an organisation's success. This, in my view, is the rather narrow way of thinking that is making our whole world unsustainable.

Yes, I agree wholeheartedly that we need our businesses to be sustainable. However, I also believe that we don't need to do so by making money our key driver. Money may be a key indicator of our sustainability but it is always a means and never an end.

I have worked with many business leaders over time and have seen the pressures this focus on increasing their earnings has brought to them and their staff ... and let's not forget their families.

Although I appreciate that money brings opportunity, it never gives meaning. Still, we all go around asking ourselves how we can earn (more) money. Me too, even though I feel I should know better!

I prefer to think of our capacity to earn money as nothing more than a direct result of having been of service in a way that creates value for all parties.

What helps me to come from a place of service is to connect to my 'why'. Why am I in business? Why am I offering what I'm offering? Why am I doing what I'm doing?

What is a sustainable business, but the graceful flow of give and receive?

Contribution is at the heart of a sustainable business.

♥

THE HEART OF GIVING

When I read that Mark Zuckerberg, founder of Facebook, announced that he was going to be donating 99% of his multibillion dollar organisation's shares to charity, I sat up and paid attention.

The fact was remarkable in itself, but what made me really sit up and take note is when I read his answer to one of the questions in the comments section. The question was, "What prompted you to give away so much of your fortune so early in your lifetime?"

His answer provided interesting food for thought. He explained that there were two reasons:

Firstly, he said, "... there is a lot to learn and giving, like anything else, takes practice to do effectively ..."

The thought that the act of giving needs practice to get right created a bit of a mulling over moment for me. But he has a point. If there is an art to receiving then there is an art to giving.

What was particularly interesting to me, though, was the use of the word 'effectively'. I have never associated that word with giving, as I see giving as an affair of the heart and 'effectiveness' as an affair of the brain. However, I suppose he may well be describing the art of sustainability here, which is a matter of balancing our heart with our head.

Secondly, he said "... any good we do will hopefully compound over time ..." And he is right, the sooner we start, the more impact we will have over time. Our offering doesn't have to be perfect, it just needs to be heartfelt.

Contribution is the art of giving and receiving.

♥

THE IRONY OF ASKING AND RECEIVING

When I was 25 I went backpacking. One of the jobs I did was knocking on doors to ask for money for a charity supporting those suffering with retinitis pigmentosa, a degenerative eye condition.

I have to admit that I didn't do this out of the goodness of my heart, or because I felt called to support this charity. In fact, I had never heard about the disease, but I was down to my last 70 Australian dollars and needed money for food and accommodation. This was a job that was available to me at a time that I needed it.

It never occurred to me then that I shouldn't be paid for the work I did. Nor did it occur to me that it may be a bad thing to be asking for money, as I assumed that the people who were suffering from this terrible disease needed the support.

What did occur to me, however, was that I should have been paid more. The job paid badly, because I was only allowed to take home a very small percentage of what I collected, and what I collected depended on how the system worked.

It quickly became clear to me that when you were dropped off in a rich area you received very little, whereas when you were dropped off in a poor area you would come away with twice as much.

There were two reasons for this. In a rich area you had to walk ten times the distance to get to the next house, and in a council estate the people had more empathy for your cause.

We all hoped we would be dropped off in a council estate.

I'm uncertain about what to conclude here, but for me this story is so full of irony on so many levels.

Perhaps it highlighted to me that those who are good at giving, aren't always good at receiving, while those who are good at receiving, aren't always good at giving. And that when you don't feel an emotional or spiritual connection to a cause, you might find yourself becoming resentful about your giving. Especially when you feel that you're not receiving the right value for the value you feel you have put in.

Contribution is giving and receiving value for what you do, whatever the currency.

♥

THE DONATION DILEMMA

When I first started to speak about Contribution being the route to long lasting happiness, one of the things I often heard was, "But I contribute so much already!" I understood this frustration as this was a feeling I also felt at times.

These days we are bombarded with requests to contribute to a good cause. Images and pleas invade our daily lives. Adverts on television and radio, posts about charity challenges on social media, all asking for donations for anything from cancer research and war victims to saving donkeys.

You cannot turn anywhere these days without a request to support a charity. You could argue that charity donations have become a hugely competitive industry.

It is such a challenge and one I have been grappling with for a while myself. Particularly since I have been talking about Contribution.

Give, give, give. It is hard not to be affected. It is hard not to be moved. We want to support all and everybody and we know we can't. So we harden our hearts, as how else are we going to survive the onslaught of guilt that we feel about 'not doing anything'.

Recently I have started to open my heart and look honestly at what feelings come up for me when giving to charity. When do I give? Do I feel that I should give, or do I actually want to give? Why do I want to give? Do I have the capacity to give? In asking myself these questions I have started to understand the difference.

Now, when I feel connected I give. When I feel guilt or stress I don't. It is still a challenge, but it has given me more understanding about how to give sustainably and with the right energy.

Giving is ultimately about how we feel, and I hate to feel that I'm being emotionally blackmailed, even for a good cause.

Contribution is giving out of love rather than guilt.

♥

BE A RAINBOW

I have had to correct myself on a number of occasions. My inner critic often pipes up about my level of Contribution.

The Art of Contribution

At times I get a little voice in my head telling me that writing about Contribution, doesn't actually make me contribute anything of value. This little voice is telling me about all those people out there who are doing amazing on-the-ground work, supporting people in the community and going out there getting their hands dirty, whereas I am just sitting in my office talking about it.

Then I have to remind myself that we all have different ways of contributing. We need to do what is right for us, rather than what we think we 'should' do.

Contribution is not a competition. It is not about who contributes what or how much. In fact, it isn't even necessarily about making a conscious effort. It is, however, about being conscious about how you show up, about doing what you love doing and spreading that around. It is even ok if you are paid for that privilege.

The late Maya Angelou knew how to put this in perspective, "Try to be a rainbow in someone's cloud." By this she meant, be a blessing to somebody.

I love coaching and learning about my subject and sharing what I have learned with others. I love spending time with my husband, friends and family. I love doing little things for people to put a smile on their face. I love singing, cuddling my dog, walking in nature and looking at a beautiful view. When I spend time doing these things I get out of my head and everything becomes lighter. That's when I feel good, and when I feel good, I sparkle, and when I sparkle I am able to add just that little bit more colour to the world.

Contribution is being a blessing to someone.

♥

JUST TWO WORDS

One of the simplest ways we can contribute in this life is by saying two words. Thank you.

I worked with a charity on their mission and vision and, amongst other things, we talked about their 'special sauce', i.e. their uniqueness. They all agreed that it was 'gratitude'. Feeling and showing gratitude for any act of kindness to their charity, in whatever shape or form.

Gratitude is a value that runs through their blood and they always remind each other not to take anything given to them, whether financial or otherwise, for granted. They make it their mission to thank people enthusiastically.

When it came down to accepting kindness themselves, however, some of them had a hard time receiving it.

This became clear during an exercise when I asked them to attribute words to each other that represented their individual 'special sauce'. Most of them were shy about accepting the beautiful words that their colleagues had gifted them.

As part of the exercise, I had asked them to read what their colleagues had said to them out loud to each other. "This is the hardest thing!" one of them called out, when it really should have been the simplest thing.

Receiving praise with gratitude requires just two words. Thank you.

Feeling gratitude is one of the simplest and most effective ways of receiving abundance. For it to flow our way we need to allow it by being open to it.

Contribution is sharing and accepting gratitude freely.

♥

UNCONDITIONAL LOVE

In a recent meditation I was reminded of something I said to my mother a very long time ago. I don't think I had ever shared this memory with anyone, until I wrote about it in my community.

I said to my mother that I didn't think I would have enough love to spare if I had children. My mother told me that it didn't work that way and that I would always have enough, but I wasn't sure. This memory made me feel rather sad, as how could I have possibly come to that conclusion?

Of course she was right, but I didn't know how love worked. I thought you only had so much to go around and at the time I felt I was running out. It was a clear sign that I had not applied sufficient self-care, as I was too busy making sure everyone else was ok. Even now I am still unlearning that behaviour.

I am also starting to understand more clearly that the more love we give, the more we receive. Love expands the moment we share it. However, you have to love yourself first and foremost. I am starting to believe that this is a universal rule.

So if we find ourselves incapable of giving our love to others, we might want to check if we have missed a step, i.e. ourselves.

To do this means forgiving ourselves for all we may or may not have done.

It means accepting ourselves because of our imperfections, rather than in spite of them.

It means loving ourselves no matter what.

If we do not follow this universal rule, then we will look to others to fill whatever hole we have left open, even though we may not do so intentionally.

Contribution is loving yourself unconditionally.

♥

CONNECT

We need the earth to ground ourselves, to reconnect us to our inner being so we can connect to others from a place of presence and grace.

I CONNECT

Through my explorations I have started to understand, at a deeper level, that the quality of our connections with others is everything.

I was once asked, "If you were to give three pieces of advice to the next generation, what would they be?"

My answer to this question was, and still is: *"Be present. Be curious. Be kind."* I call them my three keys to life, leadership and coaching.

Be present because we cannot connect fully to others until we connect to ourselves. Learning to reconnect to my inner being allowed me to connect more easily with others. This was key to being able to increase my level of Contribution to the world.

Be curious because it keeps us away from fear and judgement. When we are genuinely curious about another human being and listen with love and without an agenda, it can be freeing for both parties. Knowing that someone listens without judgement provides a safe space to share, and through our unburdening we feel relieved. Just think about what feeling relieved really means!

Be kind because kindness makes the world go round. Early in my career as a trainer and coach I learned a valuable lesson about kindness: no-one cares how much you know, until they know how much you care.

When we allow ourselves to 'be', we give permission for others to 'be' and that can be one of the greatest gifts we can give to another human being.

Reflect ♥ Recalibrate ♥ Read on

THE ECO SELF

Sometimes we get obsessed with figuring out our identity. "Who am I?" we wonder, as we look outside of ourselves to find the answer.

Through my explorations, I have learned that I was looking in the wrong direction. By looking inward I have opened up parts of myself that had been closed off and as a result I have gained a greater sense of self. My authentic self, beyond identity.

Identity, after all, is like a shapeshifter; it changes the moment our perspective changes, whereas our true self is a constant.

When I live in that authentic space, I feel powerful beyond measure. My heart knows what it wants in a way that doesn't require approval, and the need to live up to anybody else's expectations falls away.

The beauty of living an authentic life is that by being our true selves, we automatically give others permission to live in that space also. It is a space of connectedness.

Whilst musing on the subject of 'self' versus 'identity', I read a very interesting article about the 'ego self' versus the 'eco self', from which I took away the following wisdom.

When we think of the 'ego self', we think singularly, as being separate from the things around us. When we think of the 'eco self', however, we think of ourselves as being part of all the ecological systems on this earth and beyond.

This thinking is not new. Nevertheless, for me this shift of one letter created an increased sense of consciousness around the concept of our oneness. We are the trees, the ground, the rocks and the lion - we are all interrelated. When we hurt the planet we hurt ourselves and when we hurt ourselves we hurt the planet.

Sometimes the difference of a single letter makes a difference at a scale beyond our current thinking.

Contribution is knowing that we are all one.

♥

DAILY GRACE

Our surroundings are so important when it comes to our ability to reconnect with ourselves. Some need the hustle and bustle of the city, culture or music. For many of us it is the peace and quiet of the countryside and nature.

My husband and I are fortunate enough to live in a village in a beautiful setting. We moved to Devon in England two years ago, after spending ten years in Amsterdam, even though neither of us are, at heart, city people. We had starved ourselves of the very thing we needed so badly.

Whenever I enter the village I am reminded of our good fortune. The road leading into it offers the most beautiful views over the village and towards the hills of Dartmoor, a large national park, which provides a stunning backdrop. It feeds my soul and my spirit, and every time I come home I am filled with gratitude for the beauty that nature offers us. Knowing what helps me to reconnect and recharge has been key to opening myself up to receiving it.

Apart from the beauty of our surroundings, life is a little slower here. It is particularly noticeable on the roads, where basic manners still prevail. Many of the country roads are narrow and require one car to stop, allowing the other car to pass before being able to resume the journey. This often requires a bit of manoeuvring and cannot be done in a hurry. The beauty of these moments is that they always give an opportunity for gratitude. A quick acknowledgement with a smile and a wave of thanks, or a quick flash of the lights.

Occasionally we pass so close that we have to open our windows to push in our wing mirrors. More than once we've ended up laughing at one other as we shook each other's hands through the open windows before moving on.

I love these moments and I am very aware that they give me a daily opportunity to experience grace, kindness and connection, just by doing something ordinary.

Contribution is slowing down to allow ourselves to connect with our surroundings.

♥

CONNECTING LOVE

My husband appeared in my life at a time when the last thing I was looking for was a man.

I had just got out of a long-term relationship and I was ready to have some fun and some time on my own. At that time I must have given myself permission to just be me, and I realise now that the act of that is no more than an act of self-love.

In the words of Charlie Chaplin ... "As I began to love myself ... I gave those who mattered the opportunity to love me too."

Our ability to love ourselves stops our neediness. It allows us to connect from a place of love rather than need.

At the time of writing this book, my husband and I were lucky enough to celebrate our 23rd wedding anniversary. What I love about these milestones is that it allows us to reflect on how far we've come. In the context of these writings, it also allowed me to consider what Contribution means within a marriage.

Of course, like any other relationship, we have had our challenges along the way, but overall we have been a strong team. What made it so?

Looking back, I see there are several things that have been vital to the success of our marriage.

First, our commitment to communicate with an intent to understand.

Second, our commitment to staying connected by finding and retaining common ground. Particularly at times in our lives when one or the other moved in a different direction, or at a different pace. This built true companionship.

Another constant factor has been our commitment to contributing to the other person's core happiness by encouraging them to be who they are, rather than the person we might want them to be. At the same time as committing to the other's happiness, we also had to remind ourselves to remain responsible for our own happiness.

Finally, there is our commitment to continue to care. Care for each other, care about each other and care about ourselves. The moment we stop caring is the moment we give up on love.

By lucky coincidence, they are all 'C' words: commitment, communication, connection, common ground, companionship, core happiness and caring.

When you sum it all up, it boils down to a true commitment to stay connected at a heart, mind and soul level – both to ourselves and to the other person.

Contribution is learning that loving ourselves creates deeper connections.

♥

A LESSON IN LEADERSHIP

My dog, Eva, is a great teacher. She gives me the greatest joy by just being her and she is at her best when I am just being me. It is such an ongoing lesson for me.

When Eva first joined us, she was quite unruly. She was just five months old and, although she had been loved and cared for, she had been given too little in the way of exercise and boundaries.

In my efforts to be a good dog owner I had read lots of books on what would make a good dog leader. It was my job to be 'top dog', to be an 'authoritative leader who controls the pack with calm and assertive energy'. So I tried to be this person and of course Eva saw right through me.

Then one day, whilst on our way back from a walk, I had an epiphany. I had been reflecting on how miserable I had felt at failing her and I started to question this whole dog leadership thing.

Suddenly, I realised that all of the books and videos I had been consuming were written by men. Not that there is anything wrong with that, but it made me realise that all the guidance I had been given was written from a male perspective.

We all have a mix of masculine and feminine energy, but, at our core, the majority of us are mostly either one or the other. I am most definitely feminine at my core, but I have had much experience of working in predominantly male environments, so I can access my masculine energy when I need to.

However, when I LIVE there, I get stressed and unhappy and that is exactly what was happening here. I had been making myself use my masculine energy around my dog all the time, which had made me disconnect from my true self. This, in turn, meant that all my communication with her were lacking in authenticity. No wonder Eva was challenging my authority. Fake it till you make it doesn't work with dogs. They smell a f(l)ake a mile away.

So I asked myself, what energy does a strong female exude? After mulling this question over for a while, I realised that it is unconditional love, radiance and generosity. It is energy that attracts rather than pushes. As a woman, this is the energy I understand.

Yes I needed my masculine energy of certainty and firmness (rather than domination and control) but I only needed to use it when necessary.

Of course, this lesson doesn't just apply to our relationship with our dogs. We so often try to be so many things to so many people and in so many situations, that in our efforts we forget to just be who we are. In time, we even forget who we are.

We cannot influence and lead others unless we are able to lead from a place of authenticity.

Contribution is leading others by knowing who you are at your core.

♥

THE UNIVERSE IS YOUR BUSINESS PARTNER

During an inspiring conversation with fellow coach and friend Angela Barnard, around the blessings and challenges of being a 'solopreneur', she shared her insights with me.

Although we love the freedom our business gives us, many solopreneurs also feel the pressure of carrying the heavy burden of responsibility of 'making it work' all by ourselves. I definitely struggle with this at times.

Angela mentioned how, once she realised that the universe is her business partner, she knew she never had to believe that she was working alone and unsupported again.

This is such a great take on it and I have been allowing the truth of that to settle deeper in me.

Whether you believe the universe has your back or not, we are never alone, as there is always someone in our network who is in our corner.

All we have to do is to reach out to our family, our friends and connections, and allow for the support to be given to us.

Contribution is knowing you never have to shoulder your burdens alone.

♥

INSIDE OUT CONNECTIONS

I read an article in which research showed that the one thing that makes most women happy, more than all the tools and techniques in the world, are our social connections and the strength of our relationships with other people.

We all need a sense of belonging, a sense of being part of something and spending time with people you like and who like you back is very energising. This is why we will try anything to make sure that we belong.

One night, I was in the company of people that I didn't know very well yet, but liked. They, however, knew each other very well and I felt a sense of 'wanting to be part of the gang' bubbling up in me.

It was interesting to observe that I still get that familiar reaction inside, that bit that wants me to try too hard to fit in. It is an old habit created by moving around so much that I often find myself an outsider trying to become an insider.

I observed myself laughing just that little bit too loudly and feeling a little tense in my body, as if ready to pounce on a bit of information that I could latch on to. I wanted to participate in the banter and conversation, and to be seen as funny, entertaining and so on.

Of course, we can never become an insider by trying to be one, as we end up staying outside of ourselves. It is when we stay connected to ourselves that we are able to connect with others.

Contribution is connecting from the inside out.

♥

FINDING YOUR TRIBE

I spent a large proportion of my life trying to be someone I wasn't, whilst trying to work out who I really was. I know I am not alone in this, as so many of us struggle in this area.

One of the things that has helped me to connect back to my true self is finding my tribe. If truth be known, I have spent far too much time in tribes that I never fully felt part of. I pretended to be part of them, but in reality I felt like an imposter.

Recently, during a ladies networking event I was inspired by a number of women who all shared their work passionately. They dared to show up in their authentic ways despite their fears of not being good enough. Despite their fears of feeling silly.

It is interesting to me that, when we share our voice in a safe place and test it out, we can start to feel more courageous about sharing it elsewhere, as we build a stronger resilience against what knocks us down.

In the meantime, we need people to lift us up, rather than push us down. It is essential to have people in your corner who 'get you'. It is very hard to be surrounded by people who don't understand where you are coming from and where your ideas fall on deaf ears.

Although it is essential to be challenged in our thinking and our beliefs, we also need to know that, when our thoughts and beliefs are at odds with the mainstream, there are others who don't think we come from another planet.

I know my community has allowed me to share my thoughts on Contribution in a way that allowed me not to feel judged. This gave me the chance to start honing my truths around the subject, without feeling ridiculed for not having it all figured out.

Being in a safe community allowed me to experience speaking my truth, even when I was still looking for it.

There is such power in connecting with and sharing with like-minded people, as it gives you the courage to share and try out your voice.

Contribution is finding your tribe and allowing them to have your back.

♥

THE POWER OF CONVERSATION

In the course of writing about Contribution I have connected with many beautiful people.

In particular, I have met some wonderful coaches and have experienced their amazing work.

When I first moved to Devon I started a group for coaches. It was a great way to meet likeminded people in a new place.

We always started the morning with a connecting exercise where, rather than talk about what we had been doing, we shared a little bit about ourselves with each other. We shared what was showing up for us at that moment in our lives, whether a challenge, a celebration or a mixture of both.

I always liked this part. Although you only got to see a glimpse of a person's life, you often got to feel the essence of who they are.

In one of my many conversations, we explored the art of Contribution and through it I was reminded of the heart of connection. No preparation needed. No specialist knowledge needed. Just an interesting subject and a genuine curiosity and affection for each other. It's amazing what shows up when you are just having fun and spend time in that space.

What I also love about talking to people is that they always have a way of surprising you. In one of our conversations, I found out that one of the coaches in my community used to run a windsurfing club. Another runs a belly dancing group. I would never have been able to guess those activities for either of them. How our perspective of a person changes the moment we see another part of their lives!

We all have so many facets to our life and we don't always get to share them with others. It is so valuable to be given the chance to get a bit more of an insight into the tapestry of someone else's life.

In the sharing of the different aspects of ourselves we are able to weave our connections just that little bit closer.

Contribution is connecting with the essence of someone.

♥

HOME IS WHERE THE HEART IS

A poorly dog had given me an excuse to have a lazy day and as a result, I found myself watching an enjoyable Julia Roberts film called *Mona Lisa Smile*.

There was one line towards the end of the film that stood out for me, "To change for others is to lie to yourself." It gave me pause for thought as it struck a chord.

I think girls, in particular, are often trained from an early age by society to 'please others' and in that pleasing mode we often end up changing for others at the expense of ourselves. At some level, this became part of my default setting.

We start to believe that we are not good enough to be who we are. In order to be accepted, we either try just a little too hard, laugh a little too loud or try not to rock the boat by disappearing in the background when we really want to be centre stage.

Looking back I have lied a lot to myself throughout my life, although I didn't know I was doing it. All I knew was that I didn't always feel easy in myself.

Throughout my life, I have moved around regularly and this has meant that I have had to reestablish myself many times. The upside my pleasing default gave me was that I was able to be a chameleon and fit in anywhere. This gave me the capacity to read people and I learned to be adaptable and flexible, but it also came at a cost.

Changing yourself for others means you are in danger of losing yourself. Once lost, it can take a long time to find your way back.

Contribution is coming home to yourself.

♥

OUR RESPONSE ABILITY

It was the 11th of September, now commonly referred to as 9/11, reminding us every year of what happened on that terrible day when the planes struck the World Trade Centre in New York.

It also reminds me of the person I was back then. I was a yacht broker at the time and keen to do well. It was a busy day and I remember my colleague receiving a call from his mother who told him the news. I remember his shock and I recall him going onto a news site where they were streaming live pictures of the horrifying events as they unfolded.

I remember all of that, but what I remember most of all is my reaction to it. My internal response was, "This is awful, but I can't actually do anything about it and there is so much to do, I must get on with my work", so I went back to work.

Today, I cannot fathom that reaction and, since I have been reminded of it every year, I have been able to allow myself to understand where my reaction came from.

I had such a sense of responsibility. Such a need to do well. Such a need for recognition, that I had lost my perspective of what was really important to me. I had lost my connection with myself, and through it my integrity.

I realise now that, even if we cannot do anything about the events themselves, they are still worthy of our attention. Not to wallow in, but to acknowledge and send those affected our loving thoughts of compassion. So now I use my sense of responsibility in a way that is more congruent with who I really am.

Contribution is having the ability to respond with love and compassion.

♥

EMBRACING SELF CARE

I like to think that we all have secret superpowers, the very thing that gives us our inner strength. However, these powers can be drained by our 'kryptonite' - the thing that sucks all our energy and gets us to disconnect from our core power.

My kryptonite is my drive. Although drive is positive in that it helps me move forward, it doesn't always allow enough room for downtime. The thing about being driven is that it is always about *getting* somewhere and rarely about *being* somewhere. So, although it can be exhilarating, it can also be exhausting.

Self-care is vital if I don't want to burn myself out. This is a huge subject when it comes to a giver's mindset, and I still have much to learn in this area.

What does self-care look like?

When I discussed this with my coaching community, I learned that what constitutes self-care came down to personal preference. Of course, there were the basics of drinking water, breathing, eating healthy food and rest, but beyond that it was different for everyone. Whether it was walking in nature, visiting friends, meditating, sharing art, creating art, dancing, sports, singing or stroking our pets – we all had different ways of relieving our daily stresses and topping up our energy levels.

To me, self-care is ultimately about spending more time doing what gives us joy. So often, however, we don't allow time for these things, even though we know they are good for us. We come up with all sorts of reasons not to, from not being able to spare the time, to feeling we cannot spend that time on us.

The clue is in the word – SELF-care. It can only be done by ourselves! It is our responsibility to ourselves and to those around us. Without it we cannot function properly. Even though I knew that, I found that my personal wellbeing wasn't always enough reason for me to apply sufficient self-care. Knowing my 'why' beyond myself, however, helped me to leverage myself to start applying it.

Self-care is essential for a sustainable life. We cannot serve from an empty vessel.

Contribution is understanding how to apply self-care.

♥

CONNECT TO SELF

For me, singing is one of my self-care musts. After many years of not making time, I finally joined a choir last year and it has been such a blessing in so many ways.

I love it. I love everything about it. Apart from the fact that it gets me to use my voice again, which is long overdue, it is a great release for me and, at the same time, allows me to connect with some wonderful people.

What is it about singing that makes it so powerful? It is a well-known fact that singing has physical benefits. It is an aerobic activity that exercises the lungs and the heart, and it creates feel good hormones called endorphins that reduce our stress levels. Then there are the psychological benefits of people singing together, creating an increased sense of community, belonging and a shared experience. In a choir we have to listen to each other and blend our voices with one another, which means leaving our ego at the door. Singing also helps us to connect back to ourselves.

So, quite clearly, singing is great for our physical and emotional wellbeing. What is hard to measure, however, is the spiritual benefit. When the notes and harmonies hit just so, it is hard not to be lifted and moved. It's a whole different playing field and hugely underrated I feel. Singing is an international language that goes beyond words and connects us at a soul level.

Contribution is creating and being in harmony.

♥

THE MAGIC OF SELFISHNESS

Sometimes I don't want to think about others.

Sometimes I just want to think of myself.

Sometimes I just want to do nothing and laze about.

These thoughts created an internal struggle for me. Allow me to explain.

I had the idea that Contribution meant doing things and, in particular, doing things for others. This meant that, whenever I was being lazy and selfish, I believed I was not contributing and I judged myself for that.

What I realised, however, is that it wasn't laziness and selfishness that I had trouble with, but that I feared being SEEN to be lazy and selfish.

Looking at my life I think I have done and said many things to ensure that people didn't think of me as such. Why? Because it had been my emotional modus operandi to ensure people would see me as a hard worker and a giving person. Who knows, maybe this is why I have been 'so busy' talking about 'Contribution', i.e. to be seen to be anything but lazy or selfish.

I took a moment to look up the definitions of both words and the online English Oxford Dictionaries showed me the following:

"Laziness: the quality of being unwilling to work or use energy; idleness: it was sheer laziness on my part."

"Selfish: (of a person, action, or motive) lacking consideration for others; concerned chiefly with one's own personal profit or pleasure: I joined them for selfish reasons."

Wow, that nearly took my breath away. If you take a moment to think about it there is real judgement in these sentences. Such harsh words, right? No wonder our associations with these words are so negative.

But surely there is an upside to being lazy and selfish. It is our ability to be lazy and selfish that allows us to create the space we need to connect back to ourselves and recharge. We are, after all, human beings rather than human doings.

Now I am learning to be more honest with myself and I can finally accept and admit that I have always loved my lazy and selfish moments.

It is time to embrace the gifts of laziness and selfishness.

Contribution is knowing when it is time to be lazy and selfish.

♥

ARE YOU BEING SERVED?

I went to the butchers today. I don't really like going since Neil and I are both vegetarians; however, ever since we got a dog we've had a meat eater back in the house! I was on a mission to score dog bones, which is not a very lucrative purchase. Lucrative for the butcher I mean.

Normally when I go in there I feel a little bit like a fraud. A time waster. This makes me feel uncomfortable. This time, however, there was a new guy who had the biggest grin on his face and his smile didn't fade when I asked him for some offcuts of lamb bones. Nor did it change when I asked him to chop some bones a little smaller.

He did his job with such flair that I nearly wanted to start eating meat again so I could come back and shop there more often. Such is the power of service with a smile.

I also found out that all the money they received for these offcuts goes to charity. It created a double feel good whammy.

I walked away with a spring in my step.

Contribution is connecting from a place of joy.

♥

ANNIE THE TRUSTY VOLUNTEER

I was once asked what I would like my eulogy to say. This is a big question and also quite a powerful one, as it allows us to reflect on what is really important to us.

When answering this question, I realised I was not necessarily that interested in hearing about the things I had done or achieved. All I wanted is to hear is how I had made my loved ones feel and how they had felt about me.

This reminded me of Annie, who I met in a National Trust car park. For those who are not familiar, the National Trust looks after national heritage, from buildings to countryside, including many miles of the British coastline. A worthy investment for the present and the future, I feel.

Back to Annie. Annie was a membership volunteer and the local car park attendant at Cape Cornwall. Everyone who arrived received a friendly wave and a few words of encouragement delivered with a beaming smile, from, "Make sure you enjoy yourself!" or "Wonderful, I see you are already a member," to "So nice to see you again," and "Isn't it just absolutely beautiful today?"

I had been thinking of signing up with the National Trust for ages, but hadn't got around to it yet. Annie made me want to join on the spot.

Annie confided in me that she had worked as a volunteer for the Trust for more than 10 years. She shared this fact with a mixture of pride and joy showing on her face. She told me she absolutely loved her job, and was very meticulous about the paperwork when she took me through all the membership perks. I had already read up on all the facts, but I didn't want to rob her of the opportunity of sharing what she was passionate about, so I listened patiently.

After the paperwork we continued to chat. Annie had a real interest in people and before I knew it I was telling her all sorts of things, and she me.

I have experienced this so often with strangers, both in my work as a coach and in my life generally. We can talk to a complete stranger and within minutes we can feel like we are talking to a trusted friend and are willing to share our deepest secrets, even in a public space!

The Annies of this world have the ability to make people feel special when, in fact, they are the ones who are just that, special.

Contribution is having a genuine interest in others.

♥

RELATABILITY

When do we give to a cause and when do we not? What motivates us to put our hands in our pocket for charity?

As an indirect result of my interest in my subject, I have been working with and speaking to more charities and this is always an interesting challenge.

What activates people to actually hand over their money? I have been talking to several fundraisers for local charities and have heard them voice their frustration when someone chooses an overseas charity over their local one.

On reflection, I believe it comes down to three main things: Our ability to relate to the cause; our ability to relate to the people running the charity; and the impact we believe our giving will make.

First, lets look at our ability to relate to the cause. We tend to be more moved by pictures of babies, dogs and donkeys than stories about dealing with pancreatic cancer, for example. Why is this? Because we can relate to the former, but less so to the latter, unless we have had a personal experience of it. Pictures of babies, dogs and donkeys make us go gooey and tug at our heart strings, whereas stories about pancreatic cancer are less likely to hit home.

So for more people to be motivated to give their money to fighting pancreatic cancer, donors need to be given a chance to connect with the cause. What helps them to connect is a story which has the capacity to evoke an emotional response, whether by creating recognition or feelings of inspiration.

Secondly, our ability to relate to the people running the organisation. I know of three local charities whose founders have been instrumental in mobilising lots of people to freely give their time to their cause. When you ask the volunteers why they are helping their particular charity, they will tell you that it's because they were inspired by the passion of the people who run it. These founders have a natural ability to inspire and create a sense of goodwill, community and belonging.

Last but not least, the reason that people remain involved is that they can feel the impact that their giving is having. They believe they are part of something worthy and this, in turn, helps them to feel good about themselves. And let's face it, ultimately we all want to feel good about ourselves.

Contribution is connecting from a place of heartfelt inspiration.

♥

A MOMENT TO MOURN

I finally sat down to finish a story recently that I had been asked to write for a book. The story was about threshold moments – those moments in time when everything changes. I was very excited to have been asked and knew straightaway what I was going to write about.

I thought it would be easy to write my story. It turned out it wasn't and when I finally allowed myself to connect with the emotion of that moment, I ended up crying as I wrote.

The story I wanted to tell was about a time in my life when I found myself out of a job after a conflict at work – the very same event that I refer to at the start of this book.

Compared to what some people go through it was nothing. But to me, it was so unexpected and, although hindsight gave me the ability to rationalise what had happened, at the time it was a terribly painful event. I had felt misunderstood and betrayed and experienced a huge sense of loss.

I thought I had dealt with my emotions, but as I wrote about it, it was clear that, although I may have 'dealt' with them, they hadn't finished dealing with me!

I believe now, that at the time of the event, I must have worked hard on my 'state of mind', wanting to make sure that I wasn't going to wallow in self-pity. In hindsight, however, I may have inadvertently ignored my 'state of soul'. In my efforts not to feel sorry for myself and to take responsibility for the part I had played in the events, I hadn't given myself permission to mourn and allow the feelings of grief to flow out of me. Instead, they had stayed with me, slumbering in my subconscious.

Ever since my friend and fellow coach, Sue Revell, questioned if there might be a difference between our state of mind and our state of soul, I have wondered about this. I love the deeper understanding I have gained by reflecting on this distinction. We can use logic with our state of mind, but our soul doesn't understand logic, it only understands kindness.

Letting our state of mind be a gentle, rather than a forceful, companion for our soul in times of stress and trauma, will help us to let go of what doesn't serve us.

Contribution is allowing yourself the time to grieve.

♥

THE GLARINGLY OBVIOUS

I was preparing a speech on one of my favourite subjects, 'give and take'.

As I presented my first draft to my mentor, it was full of information about the findings of my research on Contribution. After listening politely, he asked me some pertinent coaching questions and quite quickly made me realise the glaringly obvious.

No one is going to connect fully with my message unless they are able to connect with me first. The only way that will happen is if I am prepared to share my personal story, rather than just my findings. Telling my story requires vulnerability and the importance of vulnerability happened to be a key factor in my findings!

It is not until I am able to connect with myself and my story that the audience is able to connect with me. It is not until the audience connects with me that they can connect with my message. It is not until the audience connects with my message that they are able to connect with themselves. It is not until they connect with themselves, that they will take away anything of value for them.

Knowing this and practising the art are two very different things.

Contribution is allowing yourself to be seen, heard and felt.

♥

THE INFORMATION AGE

We live in an information age and I feel it is an age of data overwhelm. All this access to information and knowledge doesn't always give us wisdom.

As the importance of connecting with my inner wisdom is high on my agenda, I resonated with the words of poet and critic T.S. Eliot when I read them:

"…

Where is the Life we have lost in living?

Where is the wisdom we have lost in knowledge?

Where is the knowledge we have lost in information?

…"

I wondered about what it would be like if we didn't have so much information at our fingertips. If we didn't know what was going on in the rest of the world. If we didn't read about everybody else's opinions.

It is hard for wisdom to come to us when we are constantly inundated with data. How do we pick out what is useful for us? How can we get to see the wood for the trees? How can we stop the data from blocking our inner wisdom? How do we find the wisdom in the knowledge?

I believe it requires time and space. The time to slow down and breathe. The time to sit and play. The time to reflect and do nothing. The time to connect to nature. The time to connect to our spirit. The space to rest and come back to our senses.

Even this knowledge doesn't always give me the wisdom to apply it.

So why do I feel wisdom is so key in life? Information and knowledge sends us into our heads. With knowledge does come intelligence, which allows us to connect the dots, but with wisdom comes compassion. And it is compassion that allows us to connect to our heart and our fellow beings.

Contribution is listening for our inner wisdom.

♥

LISTEN WITH YOUR HEART

I listened to Titch Nhat Hanh talking about deep listening, i.e. listening with compassion. "You listen with only one purpose: To help him or her empty their heart."

Think for a second about how often you have ever experienced being heard at this level? Truly heard, without judgement, without someone trying to fix you or the problem? As a coach I have been taught to hone my ability to listen deeply in my coaching conversations. As a coach I also know how hard this is to apply.

I distinctly remember one particular day when a coaching conversation with a new client didn't get off to a good start. After twenty minutes or so my client turned round to me and said that she felt she couldn't open up to me. When I asked her what caused her to feel that way she said, "I haven't felt 'heard", and then she added, "Not listened to. Heard!"

Wow, that was a big wake-up call for me and I knew she was right as I had not truly given her the space to just be. I was so busy wanting to help her get to a solution that I forgot my own coaching philosophy that, first and foremost, I need to be fully present with my client, not the outcome.

I asked her what would help her and she told me that what would serve her was if we could just slow down. So we slowed down and as we did the space opened up, the conversation started to flow and from that place we got a result.

I wonder what would happen if we were taught this skill as a child. Rather than just learn how to find the answers to questions and solutions to problems, we were also taught to learn to listen deeply, with compassion, without the need to have to 'do' anything.

If we all learned this from an early age, surely there would be less war, because, what is war if not a difference of perspective voiced without compassion and heard without deep listening?

Contribution is listening with compassion.

♥

Ann Skinner

CREATE

We need to be fluid, like water, and allow our creativity to flow effortlessly to and from us. We can create a life that either pushes upstream or flows downstream.

I CREATE

Apparently, ancient Egyptians believed that when you reach heaven you will be asked two questions:

"Have you found joy in your life?"

"Has your life given joy to others?"

Great questions to ask yourself before you get there.

I believe the two are intertwined. Quite simply, when we share the very thing that gives us joy we increase the joy of those around us.

Joy is our status quo. We think we need to 'get there', but actually it is a place we tend to have moved away from. So when they say, "Have you found joy in your life?" to me it means, "Have you found your way back to yourself?"

Joy and gratitude visit us when we create from a place of inspiration. Anguish and doubt visit us when we create from fear and pressure. Both have the ability to motivate us, but the journey and the end result are rather different. I would like to think that the work I put out is a reflection of my authentic joyful self, not my distorted fearful self.

Learning to be more aware of how I show up in the world and what I am putting out in the world has been instrumental in helping me to grow and contribute with more congruence.

To me, therefore, living a meaningful life means living a life of conscious and inspired creation.

♥ Reflect ♥ Recalibrate ♥ Read on

BE A REFLECTOR

I would like my work to be inspiring for others, but in my efforts to be an inspiration I have come up against some challenges. The main challenge being that we can't 'do' inspiring. We either are inspiring or we aren't.

So when are we? If there is no specific 'do', then how can we be a source for inspiration and motivation?

If there is one thing I have learned over time, particularly when I worked with leaders who needed to inspire their teams, is that you can't inspire or motivate others by telling them to get inspired and motivated!

From what I have observed, we tend to be inspiring to others when we are inspired ourselves. Only when we come from that place and what it means to us, do we seem to resonate with others.

This is one of life's paradoxes. We inspire others by becoming inspired ourselves. We motivate others by becoming motivated ourselves. By bringing out the best in ourselves we bring out the best in others.

Inspiration and motivation are infectious and create an uplifting flow of give and receive without effort, without striving. When we are inspired, we sparkle and give off an energy that is hugely magnetic. People are drawn to those who sparkle.

Be with the people you love; do what you love doing; read what you love reading; see what you love seeing; be what you love being and share that with others.

Nothing is created in a vacuum.

Contribution is being a reflector of inspiration.

♥

GREATNESS

Are you truly destined for greatness?

This question was the headline of an article I read. The question and the article itself sparked something in me, an energy in the form of irritation. We receive messages about what we 'need' to be all the time.

Be outstanding!

Be excellent!

Be virtuous!

Be the best you can be!

Be limitless!

Be …. fill in the blank …

There is nothing wrong with striving to be more of something, but sometimes this kind of thinking can be evangelised like a religion. I've been there and used these phrases too, but I see it differently now as it can be rather tiring to live up to other people's expectations of how you need to be. I am still learning to let go of this rhetoric and not judge myself for being a 'slacker'.

Also, in the question, "Are you truly destined for greatness?", is a presupposition that we aren't great already. So I wondered, what if we all stopped worrying about becoming 'great' and started to accept that we are already great, what would happen?

Would we stop creating amazing things? I don't think so. I actually think we might create even more amazing things, by working more collaboratively, without the pressure of trying to prove to others or ourselves how 'great' we are. Perhaps the best Contribution we could make to others and ourselves is by being more of who we already are, without worrying about whether we are great or not.

Whatever our destiny, whether a mother, a prison guard, a shopkeeper, a receptionist, a business director, a cleaner or a harrier jump jet pilot – we are all worthy of the term greatness.

As I am writing this, I feel a real need to stress that it is ok to have a 'normal' life. In fact, it is hugely valuable, as life can be extraordinary when it is just ordinary. That is so easily forgotten when we are pushing to stretch ourselves whilst striving for greatness.

To live a simple life by caring for what matters most might be the greatest thing you could ever do.

Contribution is knowing that we are great just as we are.

♥

HERE LIES A LEGACY

We had a lovely ramble one day, my husband, dog and I. During our walk we stumbled upon an orchard. It turned out to be a graveyard with a difference, a natural burial site.

It made us think about devoting one's life to creating a legacy. What's your legacy when you leave this earth? Sometimes that is such a weighty question. A question which can really put the wrong kind of pressure on us.

I once had a client who was so desperate to leave a legacy for his children by creating a successful business, that he found himself being stressed by spending far too many hours at work and far too little time with his children. Thankfully, he managed to change the balance when realising that his business success wasn't the ultimate legacy he was going to be leaving his children.

This natural burial site got me reflecting on whether my wish to increase my positive impact in the world is just a way of leaving a legacy. That thought felt slightly uncomfortable to me, as leaving a legacy seems to be tied to ego, whereas increasing your impact felt more about making a difference beyond ego.

Is there really a difference, I wondered, or is it just semantics?

Looking at this graveyard, where people had decided to be buried to create nutrients for a tree, I realised that this is as good a legacy as any, without ego coming into play.

Here lies Ann, she loves nature and nature loves her back.

Contribution is leaving a positive legacy.

♥

PERMISSION TO BREAK THE RULES

F*ck the rules. I say this with a smile on my face.

Life is constantly reminding me that there is only one rule and that is that there are no rules apart from the ones we are willing to accept.

Looking back on my life, it is quite clear that the times when I ignored the rules and created my own, my life moved forward in a way that inspired me.

I didn't go to university after my A-levels, as would have been expected. Instead, I chose a quick, but relevant, communications course, went travelling and attended the University of Life. This key decision resulted in an amazing kaleidoscope of experiences.

I ignored the unspoken rule not to start a relationship with someone on my boat, when taking part in a round-the-world yacht race. We have now been happily married for 23 years.

I decided to take voluntary redundancy, when it would have made more sense to stay in the safety of a job. This decision resulted in starting up my own company which allowed me to work on my own terms for the very first time.

I could go on.

All these experiences should have taught me a thing or two about rules. However, it appears I need to keep relearning the lesson, as the need to please people is strong in me. Of course, pleasing is no more than playing by someone else's rules and forgetting your own.

Now, in my current business, I am finding that many of the old rules of business don't apply. As I reinvent the rules, I am slowly finding a way to break the mould and create a new one that is a better fit for me.

Truly, there are no rules other than the ones we choose to follow.

Contribution is breaking the rules for the greater good.

♥

DON'T SETTLE OUT OF FEAR

I read an article by what has become one of my favourite writers, Elizabeth Gilbert, she of *Eat Pray Love* fame. It talks about those moments when we realise 'NOT THIS'. Not this job, relationship, life … whatever it is that comes up for you.

It reminded me of a session with a client. He wanted to leave his place of employment for very clear reasons, but had come to that point where he started to question himself. He was wondering whether he was asking too much from life and whether the job and company he was working for were 'actually really that bad'.

He had a moment where he was ready to settle. Settle for something he wasn't happy with. Settle for his 'NOT THIS'.

I knew it was his fear talking. The fear of not knowing what would come next. The fear of not being sure what his opportunities were. The fear of worrying about whether he was good enough. The fear of wanting to make sure that he could continue to pay the mortgage. I get that.

Gilbert's post describes how it requires courage to give ourselves permission to own up to our feelings of 'NOT THIS' without being totally clear on, what I have since started to call, the 'WHAT THEN'.

This doesn't mean we all immediately have to leap into the unknown and quit our job, relationship, etc. Some of us have a responsibility to those around us. However, the moment we acknowledge our 'NOT THIS' to ourselves, we have already taken a giant leap of faith that will have an impact on every decision we take from that moment on.

The 'WHAT THEN' will always take care of itself. This I totally believe with every fibre of my being.

Contribution is not to settle for anything or anyone unworthy of you or your time and dedication.

♥

THE CREATOR AND THE DESTROYER

My husband looked at us and said, "My two girls, the creator and the destroyer!"

He was referring to me and our dog, Eva. I was drawing and Eva was chewing a ball. Both happily engaged in our activities.

It made me wonder about life. Isn't that just what we are all doing? Either we are creating or we are destroying. One cannot exist without the other.

Nature is such a beautiful example of this cycle. Nature dictates that we need to destroy in order to create, as all that which has a beginning, by necessity, also has an end.

It happens around us and even in us all the time. Cells are constantly destroyed in our body and new ones are created every minute. The sun rises and sets every day. The moon waxes and wanes every month. Plants grow and die and leaves open and fall with every season.

We are energy and our energy cannot remain stagnant. Sometimes we need to destroy in order to make space for our new creations.

Contribution is knowing when it is time to destroy and when it is time to create.

♥

THE POWER OF IMPERFECTION

Much has been written about the concept of perfectionism but something struck me about this.

I used to believe I was a perfectionist, but actually I am pretty much the opposite of a perfectionist. Why? Because I don't really like working hard to perfect something at all. I never have, even though I might have displayed plenty of evidence to the contrary.

The truth? I just like messing around and doing things on instinct. I really don't mind hard work, in fact I relish it, but I don't like redoing things time and time again as I actually get bored quite easily.

The old rules that I used to live by still make me feel that this is one of my failings; that I should want to work harder at things to create perfection. The real me believes that I need to embrace this new way of being.

My writing doesn't need to be perfected. My drawing doesn't have to be perfected. My singing doesn't have to be perfected. That is not what I am about. I am an intuitive being and a lot of my work doesn't necessarily improve by reworking what has already captured the essence. This doesn't mean I don't like to improve or create a quality product; it means that I improve by playing, by trying things out. That is my preferred way.

What is very clear to me now is that the perfectionist in me was really just worried about everybody else's opinion, rather than wanting to do something really well. Believing that I was a perfectionist stopped me from being authentic in my output. The result was that it often decreased rather than increased the quality of my output.

Contribution is the ability to embrace our creative imperfections.

♥

FAKE IT TILL YOU MAKE IT

In a group exercise we were asked to answer two questions:

"Where are you still faking it?"

"How could you just be it?"

This triggered a whole philosophical debate on the subject.

When answering the question, I realised that I was still a little hung up on 'looking successful', i.e. looking like I am in control of what I am doing and that I have a financially sound business, because I believe these to be important in other people's eyes.

I remember when I first started my first training and coaching business with a friend and colleague. We used to park our beat up cars around the corner so that our clients couldn't see them and judge us. We felt it was important to be seen as a serious business partner. We also had a programme full of courses which at the time were still in the process of being created.

We faked it till we made it. Two years later, those courses were all written, although we continued to have fun in our old cars for at least another year or so.

To be quite honest, faking it gave us courage, and our belief in our pending business success helped our clients to believe it too.

What we didn't fake, however, is who we were as people and the track record of our experience. Nor did we take ourselves too seriously, and we definitely didn't tie our self-worth to our business success.

So whether we 'are it' or pretend to be it, ultimately what matters is how we FEEL about ourselves and our actions. Sometimes we need to feel as if we already 'are it' before we 'become it' but we should never lose our authentic selves in the process.

It can be a fine line and I will freely admit to not always having stayed on the right side of it.

Contribution is being you even when you are faking it.

♥

BE IT TILL YOU ARE IT

Let me expand on the subject of faking it, by bringing in a slightly different perspective on the matter.

For years I told my husband that I wasn't a writer. One day he turned round to me and said, "Stop telling yourself you aren't a writer." It was the best advice he could ever have given me. It was also a great reminder of the fact that we have to be careful what we tell ourselves, as we might start believing our own rhetoric.

This begs the question, when can you truly start calling yourself a writer, entrepreneur, leader, coach, artist, etc?

Is it when someone gives you the certificate? Is it when you have worked hard at it? Is it when you think you are good at something or is it when someone gives you the endorsement or when someone pays for your service or product?

It occurred to me that I am of the persuasion that it starts with us deciding that we ARE it. Decision, after all, is the creator of our destiny.

It reminds me of the story of Seattle's Pike Place Fish Market which is a great example of this. When business was slow, they decided to hire a consultant to help them change things around. This consultant asked them to think about what they wanted to be and they decided that they wanted to be 'World Famous'. In order to make that more real for themselves, they decided to add the words 'World Famous' to their logo before they were even close to being it. That decision, however, created the momentum and sparked the inspired action which ultimately helped them to live up to their name and eventually they became exactly that which they wanted to be - World Famous.

Perhaps it is, therefore, less of a case of 'faking it' and more a case of 'embracing it' and allowing ourselves to believe it to be true. We cannot create freely unless we allow ourselves to be all of who we are.

BE it till you ARE it is my new motto.

Contribution is embodying who you want to become.

♥

HUMBLE PIE

I came across a quote that said, "Write like it matters and it will!"

This resonated with me. At times I have been too apologetic about my writing and I realise this doesn't serve me, nor does it serve my readers. Believing that whatever you do matters is a simple but very powerful philosophy.

In my workshops on finding our secret superpower, we also took a look at our kryptonite, i.e. the thing that gets in the way of ourselves. In one of these workshops, humbleness came through as a theme. Humility is admirable, but it has a shadow side. Sometimes, in our efforts to be modest, we become apologetic for who we are to the extent that we lose ourselves and our power.

I believe it was the author C.S. Lewis who said, "True humility is not thinking less of yourself, it is thinking of yourself less."

No matter what we do in life, let's do it as if it matters, because you know what? Either way, the energy you give to it does matter.

Everything we do has an effect on what is happening around us, so why not live like it matters, because it will.

Being ourselves requires us to own our superpowers, without boasting, but also without apology.

Contribution is owning our superpowers without apology.

♥

AN AWFULLY INTERESTING NOTION

Elizabeth Gilbert writes in her book *Big Magic*, "Sometimes I think the difference between a tormented creative life and a tranquil creative life is nothing more than the difference between the word awful and the word interesting." This stopped me reading and made me jump for my computer.

I thought how 'awfully interesting' this was… and also, in my experience, quite likely to be true.

Why is it that we believe that in order to be interesting or to have something of value to offer, we need to have 'suffered'?

Buddha teaches us that pain is inevitable; suffering, however, is optional. This is, of course, the basis of mindfulness so this may be nothing new to you. Gilbert's words did, however, make me think about suffering in the context of creativity and Contribution.

When we anguish over everything we create, whether it's our work, our looks, our life, or our thoughts, we suffer. When we look at them with a curiosity detached from our ego, we feel more at peace with ourselves.

Perhaps our creativity is best served by concerning ourselves with showing interest, rather than worrying about being interesting.

Contribution is creating from a place of curiosity.

♥

THE ART OF SURRENDERING

I read a great quote by Eckhart Tolle, "Until you practice surrender, the spiritual dimension is something you read about, talk about, get excited about, write books about, think about, believe in – or don't, as the case may be. It makes no difference. Not until you surrender does it become a living reality in your life."

This reminds me of something that happened when I was taking part in a round-the-world yacht race more than 20 years ago. We were sailing from Rio de Janeiro to Hobart, Tasmania.

One of our crew members was terribly seasick – so much so that at one point we were actually fearing for his life. Unfortunately, we were only halfway, right in the middle of the Southern Ocean, many miles from anywhere and too far from land and shipping lanes for him to be taken off by either helicopter or another boat.

He had lost a huge amount of weight in a very short time and was in a bad state. Despite that, his strength of character meant that he continuously fought his feelings of seasickness and kept trying to go on deck in an effort to be useful, until he was too weak to do so.

One day, a crew member offered to pray with him. He resisted for a while, but finally surrendered and agreed. If my memory serves me correctly, it was from that moment on that he started to feel a little bit better.

I have always believed that this prayer facilitated acceptance of his situation and when he stopped resisting his seasickness, it started to ease a little.

So what does this have to do with creation? Whatever we resist persists and whatever we push pushes back. We can either create a life that pushes upstream or one that flows downstream. Surrendering to who we truly are, rather than who we feel we ought to be, is key to creating a life filled with joy, rather than struggle.

Tolle is right in that we can know this, but we don't really experience it until we live it. This has been an ongoing learning for me personally and I know that, in order to contribute fully, I need to continue to surrender to what is.

Contribution is practicing the art of surrendering.

♥

SURRENDERING TO THE MUSIC

As you may have guessed by now, letting go has been a big feature of my journey.

I thought at the beginning of the year that I was 'done with letting go' and could start to move into a year of creation. However, it seemed that in order to create I had more to learn about the power of letting go.

Singing gave me my biggest lesson.

I have always loved singing. Although I have a decent voice, I know it could be a lot better if I practiced more and, more importantly, if I dared to let go more.

When we first moved to Devon I wanted to find a choir that would suit both my ability and my personality. I finally found one which offered the mix of quality and fun I was looking for and I was happy when I passed the audition.

For our summer concert, our choir director invited us to try out gospel type mini solos, to give us the chance to stretch ourselves. Gospel is all about surrendering to the spirit of the music and it requires confident, bold brush strokes, rather than worrying about colouring within the lines.

I have always had a fear of hitting a bum note and looking silly. However, when we received this opportunity, I decided to go for it. I sang, hit quite a few bum notes, but in the end I felt happy in the knowledge that I finally dared to let go.

That moment of daring gave me more opportunities to perform. It helped me to become a better singer and to my amazement I even made it onto the choir's solo performers page.

We can surprise ourselves when we understand that we don't have to be perfect before we put ourselves out there. It is in the trial and error of the doing that we find our voice – literally and figuratively speaking.

Contribution is being prepared to show up and hit a bum note.

♥

TAKING THE EFFORT OUT

I've always found that the singing lessons I've taken are a bit of a life lesson and I fondly remember one particular lesson.

My singing teacher challenged me to really stretch myself in the higher regions and I was always worried I wouldn't be able to quite reach the top note. In anticipation, I would strain my vocal chords, which made it hard work and resulted in a shrill and tinny sound.

We took a moment to explore what was happening and it was clear that I was trying to control it. Instead, he invited me to relax, drop my jaw, trust and open up. "Just let the sound come out and then use your diaphragm to support it, not control it mind, just support it," was the advice.

It became a lot easier and the sound of my top notes filled the room.

Such a beautiful metaphor for going through life with more ease – letting go, trusting, relaxing and allowing. All of this gave me everything I needed to give more of myself more effortlessly.

Makes you think, doesn't it? When we create, we sometimes feel we need to work hard at it. We overthink things; our body contracts; we slog away to 'make it work', but when you really think about it, many of our most beautiful creations flow from us naturally, with love and grace.

Contribution is creating with effortless grace.

♥

CREATIVITY AND TIME

We all feel pressured to do more work in less time. However, creativity is not interested in time. What I mean is that creativity is not interested in working efficiently and showing up quickly. It shows up when it is given time and/or when it is time.

My niece is a good example of this theory. She is very creative and I appreciate this may be down to an innate ability, but my sister, her mother, also told me once that they deliberately allowed her to get bored. Her boredom allowed her inner creativity to come out and play.

To back up this argument, perhaps I could share the results of a research paper I read in an article. The research showed how time affects our creativity. In a simple exercise with school children, they asked them to complete a drawing of what looked like the bare bones of a clock.

First they were given just ten seconds to create their interpretation of the drawing. The result? Every single one of them finished drawing a clock with some minor variations on a theme.

Next, they were given ten minutes and the outcome was mind blowing. Everybody had created a completely different drawing, with wildly elaborate, out-of-the-box interpretations compared to their original efforts. A sense of space gave them time to play and allowed them to access their inner creativity.

This exercise is such a great example of how forcing creativity by limiting our time also limits an outcome. Efficiency isn't the same as effectiveness.

If we want to create value in and for the world, we need to be able to lean into time, breathe, slow down and allow our creativity to unfold.

Contribution is allowing our creativity to unfold in time, rather than on time.

♥

THE SPICE OF LIFE

I believe my mother always felt that, compared to the rest of us, she wasn't very creative. Since I have grown up and gained a little bit more wisdom on the subject, I know how wrong she was.

My mother was very creative. I think that she may have meant that she wasn't able to draw, write, paint, act or sing like some members of our family. These activities are generally known as the 'creative arts' but, like intelligence, creativity and artistry come in so many different packages.

When we were younger, my parents scraped all their hard earned savings together in order to buy a small, dilapidated farm. With much hard graft, enthusiasm and imagination, they created a lovely home for all of us.

My mum thrived there and had to be very creative to help make ends meet. Although she hated any kind of housework, I do believe she loved creating a home. She painted the house, created a stunning garden and a large productive vegetable plot (from which we ate all year round), made all the furnishings and many clothes. She had a real flair for colour and, amongst many things, she taught us how to spin the wool from our own sheep, colour them using natural dyes, and design and knit our own jumpers. I still have one in my cupboard today.

In those days we spent many days making things together and, right up until the end of her life, when Parkinson's had consumed much of her steady hand, you would have still occasionally found her with a needle in her hand, adapting a bit of clothing to give it just that little bit of a creative twist.

To say that you are not creative is to deny your true divine self. We are all capable of creativity.

Creativity is the spice of life.

Contribution is recognising and using our unique creative ability.

♥

HEARTRIBUTION

Did I mention that my niece is an exceptional young lady? I know that I am her aunt and that would make me biased, but hear me out.

The reason why I believe she is special is because she likes to use her creative talents to make others happy. When she was 14, she spent hours and hours in the days leading up to Christmas drawing and creating unique gifts for her parents, aunts, uncles and grandfather.

These presents were made with love and joy and were specifically created with the recipient in mind. When it was time for her to give us her gifts, the reactions on our faces mirrored hers as we opened our presents.

Mine was a lovely notebook. She had spent a great deal of time looking up quotes and copying them in the book, as well as adding beautiful drawings and pictures to help keep me inspired and encourage me to continue my writing and develop my creative ideas.

The quote on the cover was one of my favourites, "You can't use up creativity. The more you use, the more you have."

I realised that it's the same for love – the more you share your love the more you will be loved, and the more love you will have to share.

Contribution is sharing your (he)art freely.

♥

CREATIVITY AND COMPETITION

So many times I find myself wishing I was more like 'so and so' or 'so and so'. It is only a fleeting thought, because mostly I am very happy being me.

This habit of comparing ourselves is so trained into us from an early age. We have grown up in a highly competitive world and although competition has its place in the universe, I believe it is also responsible for a lack of connection, collaboration and has the ability to stifle our creativity.

A competitive drive can be a real asset when it is borne out of a will to better oneself. When competition comes from a place of ego, fear or jealousy, however, we might want to take a good look at what we're creating.

Our need for perfection is often rooted in our comparisons with others. It stops us from being creative, and from doing things for the joy of it. We cannot create from a place of flow when we constantly apply our critical thinking.

If we want things to be perfect, we will always end up striving for something more, and something more isn't always something better.

Creating more understanding about the nature of being human has allowed me to accept that our perfections are to be found in our imperfections.

Contribution is using our competitive nature to better ourselves for the greater good.

♥

SLOW DOWN TO SPEED UP

"What is the difference?" my client asked me one day when I cautioned her to slow down and set an intent rather than an outcome.

It was a great question and, although I knew the difference, it helped me to gain further clarity by formulating the distinction between the two.

When a client comes to me wanting a specific outcome, and when they are clear on the result they want and why they want it, then working on a specific outcome is totally appropriate. In this instance, their focus creates positive energy and they experience the accompanying pressure as something to be relished.

However, most of the time clients come to me with a lack of clarity about what they want. All they know is that they don't want to stay where they are. This is when I ask them to set an intent rather than an outcome. To set a wish with as much clarity as they have at their disposal at that specific moment in their lives. An intent which allows for scope and relieves the pressure of achieving a specific outcome.

Setting a specific outcome at a time like this would only result in narrowing our options. Our focus would put us on a particular path, a path that could stop us from seeing other opportunities. Opportunities that may be much better aligned with who we are and what we need.

The challenge with setting an intent rather than an outcome, however, is that it can feel rather frustrating as there is a perceived lack of control. Moving towards a clear outcome helps us to believe that we are in control of our destiny, and that it would help us to create a quick fix for our problem. The problem being our feelings of discomfort.

A quick fix, unfortunately, tends to be a temporary measure. I would also argue that making big decisions about our future from a state of frustration and confusion might not be the best remedy as it rarely invites inspired action.

In times of discomfort, I have learned to slow down and take my time to explore before heading off on a particular path. I focus my attention on acting from a sense of curiosity, rather than chasing a fixed outcome. This has helped me to create outcomes beyond my initial dreams.

Be the tortoise rather than the hare. In the long run you will get there quicker.

Contribution is slowing down to create results that are sustainable.

♥

MY WAY

I used to train people in sales and management skills, and it was always interesting to observe how different people reacted. Some were looking for the specific 'how to's'; some were resistant to learning new ways, and others were open to trying things out.

I tried to remind myself to encourage them to find out what worked for them, to use that and discard what didn't work for them.

You see, I believe there is no ONE WAY, there is only YOUR WAY. However, sometimes someone else's way can help you on your way.

I don't think we were ever meant to be the same. I believe that the whole point of life is that we are meant to be different. How else would we be able to learn from one another? It is very helpful to learn new perspectives and new ways from others but we should always remember to first check in with ourselves to see if it is something that works for us too. Sometimes that means trying something before we judge it.

Frank Sinatra sang, "I did it my way" and, whether you liked it or not, he did and through that he dominated stage and screen for many years.

Contribution is doing things your way whilst staying open to new ways.

♥

DARE TO DREAM LIGHTLY

I listened to a beautiful and heartbreaking speech from a young student who addressed his fellow pupils a week after he was diagnosed with cancer.

In it he urged his peers to stop looking at long-term dreams and start working on short-term goals. He reminded them to show up for what was in front of them and give that their all, as they would never know where it might lead.

It is the opposite of what we have been spoon fed over such a long time. That we are expected to know the answer to the question, "What is your three, five or 10 year plan?" From my background in recruitment I know that this was one of the stock questions many companies required you to be able to answer and one that only a few candidates truly knew the answer to. I believe most didn't and felt pressurised to make up their answers.

Plans and focus are brilliant for creating a productive mindset, but in the last couple of years I have started to understand that this obsession with our long-term plans can also be counterproductive.

Even when we do know the answer to this question about our vision for the future, there is a danger that we end up holding on so tightly to our dreams that we try to force them.

We forget the reality of how dreams work.

In our dreams we only gently hold the space and allow for anything to happen. Remember that in our dreams we even allow ourselves to fly.

Contribution is showing up to the moment in front of us.

♥

ENJOY THE JOURNEY

Jim Collins, author of *Good to Great* reminds us that. "Work is not a means to an end; it is an end in itself. If you create work you are deeply passionate about – because you love to do it and you believe in what it can contribute – the very act of work can become a source of sanctuary and meaning."

Even when we know this, how hard is it at times to remind ourselves to enjoy the journey as we go along? Even when our work gives us meaning, we sometimes forget to breathe, laugh and enjoy ourselves.

The moment we get fixated on outcomes, or on solving problems, or worry about 'how we are going to do it all'. We forget to feel good. Of course, when I say 'we', I mean 'I'.

What helps us through these times? Well, I have a sneaking suspicion that the answer will be around creating some solid habits that serve us. Habits, not from a place of pure willpower, but from a place of routine and love for ourselves.

One good habit to get into is to remember to always be kind to yourself, by reminding yourself that you're always doing the best you can in any given moment.

Contribution is creating worthwhile habits that serve us and the greater good.

♥

CREATION AND CONSISTENCY

Twelve months of writing gave me pause for thought and allowed me to reflect on what I had created.

366 daily stories (it was a leap year!).

80,615 words.

Number of people reached: unknown.

Number of people affected: unknown.

What I did know was that taking this consistent action turned out to be life changing for me. It helped me to become a more rounded person and, as a result, also a better coach. Unfortunately, I wasn't able to accurately measure, or even guess, what the impact on my readers had been. Nor was I able to worry about that.

The moment I tried to write specifically for the wants and needs of others, I found myself getting stuck in my head. Neither was I able to write strategically, as it stopped the joy in the act of writing and when the joy stopped, I got stuck.

So instead, I just wrote, perhaps rather selfishly, what came up for me daily, in the belief that whatever created value for me, would in some small way create value for those who chose to read it.

Apart from the fact that I enjoyed the act of reflecting and writing, my biggest enjoyment came from sharing my creative Contribution with others. It was a creative outlet which helped me to share my heart and my work in a way that felt congruent to me, without the need to aim for any specific outcome beyond my daily output.

I was also aware that doing something ordinary consistently created the opportunity for something extraordinary to happen.

When I finally finished, I allowed myself a little celebration for the fact that I had been able to commit to taking this consistent action. The moment reminded me of writer Steven Pressfield's story about when he finally finished his first book. He visited his friend and mentor to share the good news and when he expected praise and celebration, his friend told him, "Great! Now start the next one!"

The Art of Contribution

What I took away from this was not that we shouldn't celebrate and just work hard, but that the process of creation is where the real celebration is to be found.

Contribution is creating extraordinary change through taking consistent ordinary action.

♥

COMMUNICATE

We need to be aware that our very essence is like the ether - it's more than what our eyes can see. We are the energy that makes up our universe and have the power to create or destroy.

I COMMUNICATE

Over the course of the year, I have spoken to many people around the world, coaches in particular, and many have been an inspiration for me.

One of the people that I respect for the authenticity she shows in her work is coach and artist Allison Crow. Her tagline is 'share your heart, show your work'. I have always loved that, and recently I have started to think of it for myself as 'show your heart and share your work'.

It is a small distinction, but for me it means the following: It takes vulnerability to show the colour of your heart and it takes generosity of spirit to share your work.

I believe in our collective consciousness and that, once we start showing our heart and sharing our work, invisible lines are being cast out into the world that help us to connect to other hearts – the hearts of those who are meant to see and hear us.

Giving attention to our thoughts and our spoken words will help us to communicate better who we are and what we do. At the same time, understanding that our communication has the power to both create or destroy, helps us to be clearer on our intentions.

To share ourselves wisely, with integrity, lies at the heart of a sustainable world.

Through my exploration, I have increased my sense of consciousness around what I am putting out into the world in a way that adds to it rather than detracts from it.

Reflect ♥ Recalibrate ♥ Read on

THE MYTH OF THE HOLY GRAIL

The moment we find what we think is the Holy Grail to one of life's secrets we feel compelled to share it. So, we go around saying, "Listen to me! It's like this! I have the secret to finding a, b, c …"

When we wake up to a new awareness, we believe that everyone should be sipping from the same cup full of the sweet nectar of life. "Here is the thing you have been waiting for, the four steps to a successful life; three secrets to everlasting love; or the 10 things you must know about how to live a happy and abundant life!"

We share it because we believe it to be valuable and true. What I found is, however, that others' Holy Grails' often have value and often share a truth, but they are not necessarily valuable and true for all of us.

Thinking back to when I first started my explorations, you would have heard me say, "Listen to me! Giving is the route to long lasting happiness!" I shared my thoughts with whoever was willing to listen.

The thing is, although I was right, I was also wrong. It wasn't the whole story. What I learned is that what makes sense to one person can be totally wrong or confusing to another.

So how do you know what is true for you?

Over this past year, I have learned not to listen to anyone else for my truth. Paradoxically, I have also learned to be a better listener.

I have become more open and curious about other people's perspectives, whilst being more present with what resonates with me, and what doesn't.

I found that, when I created a greater sense of self, I became more internally directed. When I became more internally directed, I was more able to receive input without finding myself swayed too easily. In truth, I became less gullible.

There is so much wisdom to be gained from listening to others but only we can decide which is the Holy Grail for us.

Contribution is listening out for your truth.

♥

TRUST YOUR CURIOSITY

I started to notice that I found myself telling people that I was in danger of boring them because of my fascination with the subject of Contribution.

Why did I say this? No one had actually said that to me, nor did I bore myself with the subject. Sure, I may have had some people wondering what it was about this subject that kept me so enthralled, but nobody actually said, "Ann this is starting to bore me!"

In fact, I have had many powerful, hugely interesting and deeply connecting conversations with people as a direct result of discussing this subject and all its facets.

To find out why I was saying "I bore people" with my subject, I decided to do some self-coaching and apply my curiosity. I asked myself why I might feel the need to say this.

The only reason I could come up with was that, somehow, I felt a need to protect myself. Protect myself from judgement, which I realised meant that at some level I was actually judging myself. Reflecting on this made me understand that believing and saying that "I bore people," actually made me boring.

Getting to the heart of the matter gave me permission to let go of my need to excuse myself by pre-empting that I was a bore before someone got the chance to tell me that I was.

From that moment on, I decided to start to trust myself. Trust in my reasons for having this fascination. Trust in the fact that I don't need to be 'interesting' but 'interested'. Trust that cultivating my curiosity around the subject will be fruitful, whatever the outcome.

Contribution is exploring your fascinations.

♥

BELIEVE ALL OF THE TRUTH

So often we tend to think the worst about ourselves. Anna Pinkerton, a friend and respected colleague, talks about our 'inner brutality of thought' as part of her Kindness Incorporated methodology.

Inner brutality of thought – such a powerful phrase as that is exactly what many of us often find ourselves doing. We love beating ourselves up, taking ourselves down or swatting compliments away. We are so quick to believe our inner critic.

I came across a quote by spiritual teacher, Macrina Wiederkehr, "I will believe the truth about myself, no matter how beautiful it is." It made me wonder how much better the world would be if we started to believe the best about ourselves, rather than the worst.

Surely we cannot be a true companion to others if we cannot be a true companion to ourselves?

It reminded me of feedback I received from a client after working together for three months, "…The best investment I could have made in me! You made me realise that I count! I matter and I am worthy …"

I am not sharing this to blow my own trumpet. I am sharing this because I understood the significance of those words as that is, after all, the bottom line. We are all worthy. Every single one of us. And realising that is the greatest gift of all.

We all have little gremlins in our mind that try to trick us into believing otherwise. The moment we start giving those gremlins our attention is the moment we stop contributing to our very essence.

Learning to communicate wisely, with kindness and compassion towards both ourselves and others, starts with believing that, at our core, we are perfect just the way we are.

Contribution is choosing to believe that we are worthy.

♥

SO SORRY

I had a client who kept saying sorry. Sorry for not knowing the answer; sorry for not doing something; sorry for feeling this way; sorry for being so stupid, etcetera.

I asked her gently to stop saying 'sorry' unless she felt that there was something that she was truly feeling sorry about.

Some of us have created this habit of needing to apologise for the slightest thing. Her apologetic demeanour gave me a moment of reflection about why we might feel the need to apologise when it is not necessary to do so.

I still caught myself doing it occasionally and I realised that the main reason that I did this was to make either myself or the other person feel better. The truth is, however, that most of the time it is just noise which creates a negative energy that is draining and doesn't serve its original purpose.

In the end I came to the conclusion that we either need to show up or shut up, and only say sorry when we actually have cause to say it.

Contribution is showing up, as we are, without apology.

♥

A FEMALE TRAIT

I was at a workshop for women where, after an exercise, we were asked to share our findings in pairs. I went first, shared what had come up for me and as soon as I had done so I asked the other person to share what had come up for them.

Before she did, she stopped me and told me that I could take a bit more time and allow for my story to land.

She was right. I was so busy making sure that I wasn't taking up too much space so she would have enough time for her story, that I ended up devaluing mine.

It is such a female trait – feeling uncomfortable about taking up too much space. However, giving our power away by devaluing what we have to offer through making our story less important doesn't serve anyone.

It is good to remember that there is space enough for all of us. It is up to us to take it or leave it.

Our story matters because we all matter.

Contribution is not being afraid to take up space and allow yourself to be heard.

♥

THE POWER OF WORDS

In the summer I decided to take it easy and give myself a little bit of a break.

In the back of my mind I had allocated the time for refocusing my work. I had a number of things that were vying for my attention and, although I will never be a one trick pony, I felt pulled in too many directions.

However, I noticed that this word 'focus', although not a bad word in itself, had created some resistance in me. I had started to associate the word with a sense of "I should focus more" and part of me wanted to rebel.

Then I read a beautiful article by writer and coach Stacy Nelson, which talked about her need to take time out to help herself to recalibrate. I knew at that moment that this was the word that was far more fitting for what I needed to do.

What I needed was time out so I could recalibrate. I felt I 'had' to focus, but I knew I 'wanted' to recalibrate. I also knew that, by bringing inner alignment I would gain the outer alignment I needed to create more focus in my work.

It was so interesting to experience the profound effect that words have on us. One created resistance, while the other created opportunity. Focus was all about working towards an outcome, whereas recalibration was about setting a foundation from which a sustainable outcome would naturally flow.

When we are in a space of opportunity we are more likely to be of service to ourselves and therefore the wider community.

Contribution is choosing your words carefully.

♥

SHOWING UP

I just wrote a whole load of words. I wrote them because I felt I needed to write words, but they didn't contribute anything, so I deleted them.

Sometimes the biggest Contribution we can make is saying nothing at all. Instead, we can let the space between the words exist so that our thoughts and feelings can breathe and our inner wisdom can emerge.

…..

…..

…..

Sometimes silence can be the most powerful communicator.

Sometimes you just have to show up.

Sometimes I still need to be reminded of this.

Contribution is about showing up.

♥

THE QUALITY OF OUR CONTRIBUTION

Of course, we don't all have to go out with the intent to change the world. We can, but we don't have to.

But even if we do not have the intent, we are always having an effect, as every action or non-action will contribute to something.

As renowned primatologist, Jane Goodall, said, "You cannot go through a single day without having an impact on the world around you. What you do makes a difference, and you have to decide what kind of difference you want to make."

So if we want our difference to be a positive one, rather than a negative one, we can just simply start with observing our thoughts.

As our actions are fed by our thoughts and our thoughts have the ability to create or destroy, we can begin to make a difference by choosing our thoughts more wisely.

As we create more awareness, we start to recognise which thoughts make us feel good and which make us feel bad. Once we are more able to pay attention to the thoughts that make us feel good, we can even decide to share our good feelings with others. The beauty is that, when we do, we receive even more good feelings in return.

These days I am, therefore, careful about what information I feed myself with, as I know it will directly influence what I put out in the world. If I allow rubbish to pour in, I am more than likely allowing rubbish to pour out.

Be the difference whenever and wherever you can, by learning to observe and choose the thoughts that create more value for all parties.

Contribution is creating and acting on quality thoughts.

♥

THE HEART OF SALES

I found myself being cleverly drawn in by a 'perfect' marketing strategy and signed up for an online product. I was hopeful that it might prove to be useful.

It was a clear example of buying into something that I thought I wanted, but, after receiving the offered programme, I couldn't help but feel disappointed. What we need and what we want are two very different things.

I didn't exactly feel cheated, but I did feel like I had cheated myself.

What was being offered wasn't necessarily bad, but I just couldn't connect with it. All I heard was the sales talk that was wrapped around the product and this was drowning out the possible value it may have offered me. I mentally and physically switched off and, although I felt disappointment, I also felt relief.

Relief because it was a great reminder to myself that I have evolved. I need something more spiritual. Something that feeds my deeper need for connection and is offered to me in a way that allows me to actually think for myself.

It reminded me of some of the resistance I received to the term 'sales', when I was a sales trainer and coach. Sales, unfortunately, has become a dirty word to many people. It can conjure up images of manipulative behaviour which aims to get someone to do something they don't want to do.

And yes, that happens. However, it doesn't have to happen and it doesn't always happen.

The real key to selling is sharing. Share what you believe in, share what you have to offer, but also share your time, your curiosity, your presence and your generosity. If what you offer matches what the other person needs, then the buying of your service or product is a logical result.

At the heart of sales lies our ability to be congruent and for us to be congruent we need to have a sense of Self with a capital S.

A sense of Self means a sense of service, as well as a sense of self-worth. Put those two together and you are talking about a sustainable flow of give and receive.

Contribution is sharing with passion what you can offer the world.

♥

BE YOUR OWN AUTHORITY

I had been tying myself in knots trying to find a way to offer my service in a way that felt congruent to me. I found that I still felt hampered by some old schools of thought around how I should sell and market myself in order for me to grow my coaching business.

This feeling came to a head when I found a big stick on my dog walk. I felt compelled to pick it up and, in an effort to lose some of my pent-up frustration, I proceeded to beat the ground in front of me. I kept saying, "I won't do it! I will not pander to what people want to hear in order to get what I want. If I do that, I am no better than a politician trying to get elected to get into power."

Following my outburst, I decided to share what had happened in an edgy, vulnerable video on my personal Facebook page. After I posted it, part of me immediately wanted to delete it and the other part said, "What's the worst that could happen?" I decided to be brave and leave it.

Apart from the fact that I felt liberated after sharing my personal frustration, what was interesting to me was the response my outburst had created in others. It gave me an interesting life lesson.

Although many applauded my message and my bravery for sharing it so vulnerably, there were also some who didn't understand it. Some worried about my sanity; some just couldn't connect with what I was referring to; and others felt the need to protect me by telling me that I was better off keeping these thoughts to myself for fear of "what people might think."

What I saw quite clearly at that moment was that none of their responses had anything to do with me. Their reactions just reflected where they were at in their respective lives.

For me, though, this act of sharing my honest thoughts and feelings helped me to reconnect with my message in a way that felt authentic. At the same time it helped me to reach those who needed to hear what I had to say and this, in turn, allowed them to share their honest thoughts also.

Contribution is sharing your truth as you see it, whilst leaving others room for theirs.

♥

THE SCARCITY DILEMMA

A popular marketing strategy is creating a feeling of scarcity.

Scarcity creates demand, which is why it is so effective. Why does it work so well? Scarcity creates a fear of losing out and fear has the power to get us to move into action.

However, fear in this context creates negative energy and I generally prefer to be a creator of positive energy.

When I was writing marketing copy for a workshop I was running, this thought came up as I was worrying about my wording. I wanted to share that there were limited spaces. "Will it create fear?" I wondered, "Will it be seen as a marketing ploy to get people to 'buy now'?"

These thoughts were challenging me.

In the end I realised I just had to tell the truth. There were only a few seats available. The message was congruent.

Contribution is being truthful with your message.

♥

INFLUENCING CHOICE

I had to buy a new garden fork, because the one I had been using broke during a vigorous fight with some old tree roots that I had been trying to uproot. As I stood in front of the selection in the store I was a little confused. How would I recognise a good garden fork?

As with any buying process, there are three main things that usually influence our choice: Time, Quality and Cost.

Urgency would make me buy that day, rather than go back and research further. Quality came in second, as I had just broken my other one and I wanted it to last. Cost came in a close third, as I also needed to watch my pennies.

After much deliberation, I finally managed to cut down my choices to two options. I found myself going back and forth until I read the labels more closely. There turned out to be a fourth factor that influenced my choice: Social Responsibility.

One of the two, the slightly more expensive one, was produced by a subsidiary of Kew, the Royal Botanic Gardens in London. Apart from the fact that I felt I could trust their judgement, it also came with the promise, "Every purchase ensures a contribution towards Kew's vital work."

Apart from a beautiful botanical garden, Kew is a world leader in plant science and conservation. I felt good buying this product as I knew that, in a very small way, I would be supporting a worthy cause.

Following my purchase, I read an article that confirmed my buying process. It said that, "… As consumers' awareness about global social issues continues to grow, so does the importance these customers place on corporate social responsibility (CSR) when choosing where to shop …"

I wondered what would happen if all products and services were offered in a way that would allow us to connect with their unique 'social why'.

Contribution is offering our products and services with a social conscience.

♥

THE POWER OF AN EXPERIENCE

I was talking to a fellow coach about 'honing my message' regarding Contribution, as I still felt I was standing on shifting sand when I talked about it. My message changed depending on where and who I was with and what I felt like at that moment in time.

If I was clear on what I meant by Contribution, how could I then condense that message into one short but powerful sentence that resonated both with me and the listener?

'Contribution is the route to long-lasting happiness'? 'Contribution starts with receiving'? 'Contribution is sharing the best of you'? 'We cannot contribute without receiving'? ... It all felt a little 'meh' to me and lacked power and, therefore, my conviction.

I found that the challenge with explaining Contribution is similar to the challenge of explaining coaching. Both coaching and Contribution are 'concepts' that need to be experienced, rather than talked about, to be fully understood. So how to communicate my message?

Even though I still found myself on shaky ground with regards to my communication around the subject of Contribution, I decided to put myself out there and share what I knew, whether I felt ready or not.

Sometimes we have to jump before we are ready and then let the universe take care of the rest. One thing is certain – we are unlikely to contribute anything worthwhile if we just stay in our heads worrying about it.

As writer and coach Stacy Nelson says, "Share what you are about by 'loving on' people." I love that expression and it helps me to remember to get out of the way of myself and share what I'm about by just being me.

Contribution is giving someone an experience of who you are.

♥

SPEAK TO BE HEARD

I received a profound lesson one day. I realised I didn't have to be excellent at something in order to be good at something.

I was preparing a speech and I found I was fighting an internal struggle. I was worried that my story wasn't suitable for the audience I was addressing, so I decided to make some last minute changes.

It is a fine line we walk when we want to be on message and on purpose, whilst remembering that there is no point sharing it with words that your audience won't be able to hear.

However, my internal struggle wasn't about making the changes, but about the fact that these last minute changes meant that I now didn't feel as well prepared as I would have liked to. I felt that I needed the safety of my notes and I was disappointed with myself for needing notes. Somewhere along the line I had created a rule that told me that 'excellent' speakers don't use notes.

I know it is sad that I have to own up to this. In my defence, when you have spent a bit of time in the personal development arena, you can find yourself being bombarded with messages of striving for excellence. It is the kind of pressure that can create more anxiety in a person than is necessary.

Although I don't subscribe so much to many of these ideals anymore, I still find myself being influenced by my internal drive for 'excellence'.

The lesson I received this particular morning was that it didn't matter whether I had my notes or not. What mattered was that I had done enough work to help me feel comfortable enough to share what I wanted to share in a heartfelt and genuine way; in a way that would create value for the audience.

I learned that I didn't need to be 'excellent'. I just needed to come from a place of wanting to share and contribute.

It turns out that this approach nurtures excellence in a way that is in line with who we are.

Contribution is heartfelt sharing.

♥

IN THE STYLE OF ... YOU

How often are we looking for something we have already found?

My explorations around the Art of Contribution went hand-in-hand with my personal journey to find my authentic voice. This quest turned out to be not only a figurative one, but also a literal one.

After joining the choir, I decided to take up singing lessons again. The teacher I went to was a well-respected former opera singer and as we worked together he recognised some potential in my voice.

After our first couple of lessons I noticed that some feelings of resistance had started to bubble up in me. Although I loved his teaching style, I was given songs that encouraged a certain musical style that I felt an involuntary allergic reaction to!

The strength of my reaction surprised me. Whereas before I may have ignored it and accepted whatever my teacher gave me, not this time. My feelings made it very clear to me that I didn't want to be singing in the 'style of' opera, blues, choral, rock, country or even folk (all of which I love by the way). Instead I wanted to sing in the style of, well, ME!

I wanted to explore my voice and my way and, once I realised what I wanted, I was able to make my intentions clear to my teacher. It gave him an interesting challenge and I felt suitably stubborn.

As I used to enjoy writing the odd song now and then, I also decided to listen to some of my old recordings, and what I heard surprised me. I had been looking for my voice, and realised it had been there all along. I just hadn't recognised it as I had been too busy worrying about what others thought, or what I imagined they might have thought. Or perhaps I had been wishing for what I would rather sound like.

Now I could finally accept that I sounded like me and that I decided I actually liked the sound of me.

Contribution is appreciating and sharing your unique voice.

♥

ABRACADABRA

I was reminded of the original meaning of the word abracadabra in a video by coach and entrepreneur John P Morgan, "I create as I speak."

As I watched the video, a little memory popped into my head. At the beginning of 2016 we were invited to a birthday party. At the party, the host gave us all a piece of paper and asked us to write down our wish for the year. All the wishes went into a bowl and afterwards they were read aloud, one by one.

There were so many things I could have wished for, but I had only written down two words.

A Book.

Although there were only two words, they stood for so much more. A book meant that I could offer something concrete, something tangible to the world. A book meant that I had created something of value to me which, in turn, could offer value to others. A book would represent the love I had gained for the act of writing by practicing the art daily. A book would even mean the possibility of more books.

A book could create possibilities for other opportunities to come my way. Opportunities that could help me to continue to fulfil my mission – to illuminate and inspire people to live a life that works towards the greater good.

So, you can imagine it meant a lot. But still, secretly I wondered if I was actually going to be able to write and publish it that same year as it seemed more realistic with a longer timeframe. As the year progressed, I held this dream gently, without giving the end result any real attention. Then, in the middle of August, just days from finishing my yearlong challenge, I was offered an opportunity out of the blue.

It was the opportunity I needed and I decided to embrace it wholeheartedly and allow it to help me make my dream come true.

The moment we dare to speak our dreams aloud is the moment we start making our dreams a reality.

When we do, something magical happens to us and for us. I have witnessed this time and again. The very act of speaking our dreams aloud starts to create a suspicion that it might actually be possible, even if we don't quite believe it yet!

Those that hear us rally round to help us and this, in turn, forges our belief. As our belief grows, the universe works to support us by sending opportunities our way. Our eyes have opened enough to start seeing and recognising these opportunities when they arrive. Our heightened senses allow us to trust our intuition, and our intuition will give us a nudge and the courage to jump when it is time to do so.

Abracadabra! Words really are magical, although the real magic lies, of course, in the meaning we give those words.

Don't keep your dreams to yourself. Share them openly with those who have your best interests at heart, and that includes you!

You never know what might happen.

Contribution is speaking your dreams aloud.

♥

4. CONCLUDE

CONTRIBUTION IS

In short, the 5 components of *Commit, Contribute, Connect, Create* and *Communicate* can be summed up as follows:

Contribution is committing to ourselves and a cause bigger than us.

Contribution is being clear on our giving and receiving boundaries.

Contribution is knowing that we are all one.

Contribution is living a life of conscious and inspired creation.

Contribution is choosing our words wisely.

FINAL REFLECTIONS

I was once told there are two types of people: those that get up in the morning and think, "What can the world do for me?" and those that get up and think, "What can I do for the world?"

Now I believe that there is a third question we might be better off asking ourselves: "What can I do for me that also serves the greater good?" and specifically in that order, from the inside out.

Through my explorations I've come to realise that, at the bottom of every answer to the questions I've asked around the subject of Contribution, is love. The simple truth is that Contribution means to come from a place of love. However, in order for us to fully comprehend what this means for us personally, we need to uncover and learn to love the different facets that make us who we are.

Having read my musings on the subject of Contribution, I wonder what has been of value for you.

What has given you pause for thought?

What has resonated with you?

What possible insights have you gained?

Your own reflections and realisations are by far the most powerful. At the same time, I also recognise that it might be helpful to share my key learnings with you here, as a simple reminder and an easy point of reference.

MY KEY LEARNS

- I have started to believe that in order to live a meaningful life we need to live an authentic life. A life where we understand that we are enough just as we are, and that we do not need to do or be anything to be worthy. It isn't necessarily our job to 'be good' or 'do good'. It is our job to be ourselves, as much as we can be and to do the best we can in any given moment.

The Art of Contribution

- I have learned that, when we come from a place of authenticity, we are able to impact the world positively, without having to 'do' anything, unless, of course, we feel called to. Not called from a place of feeling that some things in the world need 'fixing', but from a place of wanting to add joy to it.

- I now understand that, in order for people to truly connect with me, I first need to be able to connect with myself and allow myself to be vulnerable. Because, how can others be able to see me if I do not allow myself to be seen?

- I have started to see that our biggest Contribution to each other is to notice one another, see the beauty in each other and be there for one another, whenever we can. In order for us to be able to do that, we need to learn to be there for ourselves too. That is our social responsibility, to be a companion to ourselves first and foremost, so we can be a better companion to those around us.

- It has been freeing to learn that we do not have to give more, to be more. We do not have to do more, to be more. In fact, sometimes we even need to do less, to be able to do more. The very fact that we exist means that we are Contributing to the world in our own unique way. Indian sage, Ramana Maharshi, wrote, "Your own self-realisation is the greatest service you can render to the world."

- I have started to appreciate that it is ok to be a little bit more selfish and lazy. In fact, I would even go as far as to say that it is an essential part of Contribution. When we slow down and replenish, we allow ourselves to come back to our centre and from that place we can continue to give more sustainably.

- I have learned that our biggest Contribution is to be unapologetically ourselves. That it is essential that we embrace all of ourselves; our amazingness, our flaws, our idiosyncrasies, our genius and our innocence. To accept that I am human and that I can show all of me – curious, loving, witty and wise, but also feisty, passionate and, at times, a little too competitive or overenthusiastic in the sharing of my ideas and ideals.

- I have created awareness around which rules to accept in my life and which to let go of. I am limiting my 'shoulds' and instead have learned more about what gives me joy regardless of rules. I now know that sharing that which brings me joy with those that may benefit from it, also increases my joy.

- I have also learned that my courage came from making a commitment. A commitment to a cause, which was really a commitment to myself and to my chosen path.

- I have also learned that giving is not just a question of the heart. In order for us to create a sustainable life for ourselves and others, we also need to use our intelligence.

I want to leave us with an important thought.

It is the small things that make the big things happen. This is a message that I want to keep close to my heart, to remind me that it doesn't take much to be the difference.

And as a final reminder to myself:

Slow down ...

speak your dreams into being ...

trust in yourself and the universe ...

let go of expectations ...

work consistently on your creations ...

maintain an open but determined mindset ...

hold your vision lightly as it develops and expands ...

and remember to love and have fun.

I am a Contributionist.

ACKNOWLEDGEMENTS

To all of you who have contributed so much to my life!

We never travel alone. This book would not have been written if it wasn't for the love and support of so many people.

My total respect and gratitude goes to my friends and colleagues in the Tribe of Miracles. Thank you for sharing your dreams and challenges and thanks for being, laughing and crying with me on my journey. Every one of you has been a huge inspiration to me and I love you all!

I especially want to thank David Taylor, whose questions were the catalyst for my year-long challenge and who, at the end of my 365 days, gently nudged me to do one more day by reminding me that it was a leap year, i.e. 366 days!

Thank you also to my local Coach to Contribute community. Our monthly get togethers gave me such a sense of connection and belonging. Our honest sharing and support allowed me to find the courage to share my voice further afield.

Apart from my clients, who have been a never ending source of inspiration, I will never forget all of my friends across the world who were with me as I posted my daily musings in my online community. Thank you for your support, your comments, your thoughts, your questions and your wisdom. Thank you also to the many who read my posts in private. I feel blessed that I got to know so many of you throughout the year and know I have become a better person because of it.

I am very appreciative of those who gave their time to read earlier drafts of this book and gave me their valuable feedback. You all helped to make it a better book. Special thanks go to Kate Duggan who helped me to spot the rogue typos that crept in and questioned some dodgy bits - your work was both efficient and effective! Any errors remaining are entirely down to me!

A big shout out to all those inspirational writers and speakers who have had the courage to share their heart and wisdom with us. Some books that have made a lasting impact on me include: *Give and Take* by Adam Grant, *The War of Art* by Steven Pressfield, *Coming Home* by Dicken Bettinger and Natasha Swerdloff, *The Law of Attraction* by Esther and Jerry Hicks, *Light is the New Black* by Rebecca Campbell, *Daring Greatly* by Brené Brown, *Thrive* by Ariana Huffington and last, but not least, one of my favourites, *Big Magic* by Elizabeth Gilbert. One day I hope that I might get to swap some wisdom with some of you personally and, talking about speaking your dreams aloud, Oprah Winfrey, just say the word!

Thank you cuddles go to my dog, Eva, who has been witness to many of my musings as I grabbed for my phone to record yet another little thought snippet whilst traipsing around the woods on our daily walks.

And most importantly ….

I want to thank my family for their constant love and encouragement and, in particular, I want to express my gratitude to my husband, Neil, whose love and devotion to me, and total belief in me, has allowed me to become more of who I am.

Thank you for being a sounding board, for sharing your wisdom and your honesty.

Thank you for believing in my work at times when I forgot to believe in it myself.

You are my true companion.

5. CREATOR

ABOUT THE AUTHOR

Ann's stubborn fascination with why we do what we do developed her ongoing passion for coaching, teaching and writing.

Following a year-long exploration of the subject of Contribution, Ann founded The Contribution Evolution. Her heartfelt work encourages people to reconnect with their inner companions of wisdom and courage, helping them to live an authentic and meaningful life.

Ann is also creator of The Contributionist, a creative outlet for her expressive drawings and doodles, which she refers to as her 'HeArtwork'.

Her previous experience includes a full and varied international career in PR, sales, recruitment and people development. She also found time to go on a number of extended travel and sailing adventures, including a round-the-world yacht race, where she met her husband.

Originally from The Netherlands, Ann now lives with her husband and dog in the beautiful English countryside.

Ann's mission: To illuminate and inspire all that works towards the greater good.

Ann Skinner

BE A CONTRIBUTIONIST

There is no one way, there is only YOUR way.

Please accept **MY FREE GIFT TO YOU!**

Find your secret superpower and connect with your inner companions of courage and wisdom.

Sign up for my Free *Embrace Your Inner Superhero* guide by visiting the following link:

www.TheContributionEvolution.com/Courage

Made in the USA
Lexington, KY
23 April 2017